Happiness is the legacy of love

Love Legacy

Reem Ahmed

PASSIONPRENEUR®
PUBLISHING

Publishing information
Publishing, design, and production facilitated by
Passionpreneur Publishing, A division of Passionpreneur
Organization Pty Ltd, ABN: 48640637529

www.PassionpreneurPublishing.com
Melbourne, VIC | Australia

To the loveliest parents on Earth,
Mohamed Ismail Ahmed and Fatema Subhi Abdul Salam,
without whom I would have never become the person I am now.
I am grateful for everything you offered me! And I love you.

Testimonials

Andjou Armel Mea

The experience was amazing. I started the sessions before my position was made redundant at Emirates. However, the sessions taken helped me deal with my redundancy...I now have my goal set and I am achieving it. If anything will stop me, it is me. Thanks to God because I could meet an amazing coach like Reem who took me from the dark thoughts causing a wall in my life to a more driven and goal-oriented person. Thank you, Reem, once again, and I pray that you continue to bring change to many lives

Maya Abbas

Reem Ahmed is a professional coach, the sessions I had with her were so helpful, and the results are clearly great! Reem Ahmed coached me on "commitment" goal, which was mainly about being committed to tasks with positivity, focused mind, persistence, and becoming stronger in facing obstacles and negativity around me. The result obtained from this coaching was that I stopped complaining, moved forward, blocked negativity and negative people around me, and got committed to my goal and tasks.

Ramez Mohamed

Coach Reem is a unique coach with special creative tools that helped me a lot to find myself and see myself in the mirror to find the real person I am.

Rangana Gunathilaka

I am so honoured to meet Reem. She coached the team of SPLINT program and helped the team to balance work and private lives. Her coaching helped to define core values, improve autonomy, work collaboratively and get maximum output from the invested time. She transformed the members into an interactive and collaborative team with operational excellence with the most admirable discipline within a few sessions. Following her coaching, I was able to bring up my small idea to reach the enterprise-wide recognized program. I recommend Reem as the must-have coach on your director board or as an advocate for the start-ups if you have a genuine desire to see the success of your journey.

Mo'men Ismail

Coach Reem introduced me to myself again, I was very comfortable from the first session and it is rare thing for me to quickly trust a person and talk to him/her about everything. I thank coach Reem for listening to me and helping me to succeed in balancing the four energies, energy of soul, mind, body and emotions. She taught me to control my thoughts, and how positive thinking leads to positive action and positive results. Every time I remember her words, I feel energized to continue again. I thank her and feel really happy to know her, I thank God for knowing her and feel grateful to the person who introduced me to coach Reem, and for our communications. And that she was and still is one of the major reasons for my change. Thank you very much coach Reem.

Heba
Coach Reem is the easy-to-do coach...She delves into the depth with kindness and ease without letting you feel it...and illuminates your hidden jewels with the touch of her charming questions. I enjoyed being coached by her. And whoever has not tried it is losing a lot.

Martin Klaver
I got to know Reem as a curious and inquisitive person. Try to understand and then apply to her situation or context she is in. She is not afraid to take a critical look at herself, an aspect that I appreciate very much. In my contacts with her, she has shown an intelligent and analytical way of thinking.

Mira khatib
Reem Ahmed is one of the contributors at Arab Woman Platform. Her writing style is one of simplicity yet captivating. Her articles are thought provoking and articulate and are some of the best reads on our site. She is very professional in her dealings and abides to deadlines. A compassionate and hardworking young woman.

Muhammad Yasir Arslan
Reem as a human and as a professional is genuine and devoted. She is a versatile engineer with the ability to perform multitasking. Her strength is report writing and team building. I have found her kind-hearted and dedicated in her daily work.

Table of Contents

Acknowledgements

I thank and acknowledge my four sisters (Rajaa, Faten, Wissam, and Faihaa) and my four brothers (Nahed, Raed, Manar, and Ismail) for all the humps we endured together without allowing it to tear us apart. And for welcoming my new ideas and being willing to transform with me. With a very special thanks to my brother and dearest friend "Ismail" who has always got my back whenever I need him.

I also thank my brother-in-law, Nabil Kassem, for his continuous support, for being a big fan of my work, and for reading all my writings! I acknowledge my sisters-in-law, Noor Abdulsamad and Huda Hawarna, for their continuous support to my business. Thanks to all my nieces and nephews who were my great teachers. As I watched their behaviours from being infants to grown up teenagers and adults, I learned a lot about human beings.

Thanks to my friend and support queen, Mariam Mostafa, for her persistent encouragement during my writing journey of this book. Mariam followed up with me and celebrated my progress consistently. She kept bringing my focus back on the book whenever I got distracted. She had a vital role in making this book becoming a reality.

Thanks to my peer authors, Rodayna Tiraoui and Mona Shibel, for their support and for being there for me whenever I needed them. And thanks to my ex-colleague, Dejla Al-Amri, for being at my back whenever I needed some advice, while surviving a strongly toxic environment in my previous job.

A very special thanks to my life coach, Henda Pretorius, who supported me even after our coaching ended and offered me the very first masterpiece of this book, the story of her parents Nico and Alta. It was a nice gift that increased my appetite for writing! It gave me hope and a great vision for this book.

Thanks to my twin soul, Lina Taher Sharara, for being a cornerstone in my life for several years. Lina is a friend, a sister, a twin soul, a mentor, a teacher, and many other things I can't find the right name for. Lina has loved me unconditionally since she saw me praying in 2007. I got surprised to know that someone would love me as they see me paying! She believed in me when I was at the lowest points in my life and never gave up on me.

Thanks to my second twin soul and sister, Dr Saya Pareeth, who embraced me under her wings for many years, with all the team in her centre (The Healers) where I felt like a VIP. Thanks for being such a great doctor, one who was always available and helped my health to improve tremendously. I wish I could thank you enough, Dr Saya, because you will always deserve more. And thanks to your husband, Dr Hafeel, for his great support.

I acknowledge and thank my dearest life-time mentor, Aznive Tossounian, for her patience, for never leaving me enduring pain alone during my transformation journey, and for offering me her love unconditionally. I acknowledge my lovely mentor, Dr Shobana Pisharody, who is always available to listen to whatever I am going to share, without judgment or enforcing her opinions. With Dr Shobana I experienced full freedom. And thanks to my professional ICF mentor coach Mahmoud Abu Zaid, who supported me until I got my ACC, and beyond.

Thanks to Sharon Loeschen for forming such a great institution (Virginia Satir Global Network), for being so genuine in transferring the valuable knowledge of Virginia Satir as Virginia desired and adding to it. I remember telling Sharon "I feel as I am interviewing you that I am talking to someone so high and big." She modestly replied "No, I am just a human like you, I have two legs and two hands, just like you." It blew my mind! I wondered; how much better our world would be if more people operated with such a modest attitude from their high positions?

Thanks to the diamond that appeared in my life, who became with her kindness and fine morale a very important person in it, Dr Amira Gharib. She adopted my whole family when COVID-19 hit our home and treated the case of my sister when she was in the ICU as if she was her own sister. She supported the case with her husband, Dr Mohamed, who is a specialist in intensive care cases of COVID-19 in Egypt, from a very far distance. They supported me with information and followed up with me on Rajaa's case every single day. No words of thanks are enough to you and your husband, Dr Amira.

Thanks to the lovely illustrator Amy Sulistya, for taking all my feedback with patience and a positive attitude, and for making the exercises of this book lively and fun to follow with her illustrations. Lots of thanks to my author-coach, Clare McIvor, for her professional guidance, and for upgrading my writing in this book and making it look the way I would like any precious present I am offering others to appear. Classy, neat and gorgeous. Thanks to everyone who offered his/her true story to be part of this book, to educate people and give them hope that love is there. When utilized, it can beat any obstacle in life.

Thanks to the Passionpreneur team members, Aashish Jayaraman and Venessa Marrama for their efforts in making this book become true. Special thanks to the graphic designer who designed my book's cover. It represents my spirit and speaks out my story. Thanks to all my friends, mentors, coaches, teachers, writers of books I read, and healers for their contribution to my life. And thanks to all my clients and readers of this book for allowing me to be part of their journey in life.

Thanks to Onlinist Web Design and Marketing team, for their extensive work on my website, and for helping me in reaching out to my audience. Great thanks to the creative marketer, Ramez Shehata, for all his work and for his continuous support despite any conditions. And lots of thanks to the passionate entrepreneur, Ahmed Salem Amer, for his support and all valuable inputs and suggestions on my website and business.

A big thanks to myself (Reem Ahmed) for being with me my entire life, during good times as well as bad times. Thanks for picking me up whenever I fell down, pondering on the lessons learned, and moving forward towards a much happier and more peaceful life.

And most important of all, thanks to (Allah), our creator, for creating me, making me the person I am today, giving me the gift of writing, putting all those people in my life, and crafting my journey and whole life in a magnificently delicate way.

Introduction

*"If you don't set yourself free of your doubts and
fears, you'll never discover how marvellous your
life can be without them...coach Reem helped me to
know myself again..."*

— MO'AMEN ISMAIL

To my dear reader, I acknowledge you for taking a
courageous step to regain your birth-right freedoms. These
are the freedom to see and hear what is happening, rather than
what you have been told; to feel your feelings no matter how
ugly others may consider them, as all kinds of emotions are
powerful; to express your true self honestly and congruently;
to have your voice and ask for what you want before seeking
permission, whether it is asking for support, a promotion,
or even a form of communication that you prefer; and the
freedom to take risks and seek change without hesitation.

I am an advocate for love and peace, and so passionate
about infusing more of both into the world. I believe that by
doing this, we are contributing to healing the world from its
overlapping trauma, through unconditional acceptance for
ourselves and others.

This book is a natural product of my background, diverse
experiences, and the number of hurdles I was exposed to, in
my own life and while helping others through coaching. I am

passing all the knowledge I have gained from them to you. I want to help individuals, couples and families who value love and aspire to have more of it in their lives. This book has been written for those who understand how loving themselves affects their sense of self-worth, to support them in building healthy boundaries and defining the ways they want to be treated. Those who treat themselves with care will apply similar standards in giving and receiving love from others.

The benefits of this book will come to those willing to connect with themselves and develop the required awareness of what is happening in their inner world each moment, affecting their whole life. This connection can only happen through love. You will know how meaningful your life can be when flooded with love, to the point that you can start pouring it into the relationships with people in your life.

To my beloved readers, I want to help you avoid going through the pain I went through, to stop living in continuous misunderstanding and fear, and to release unhealthy coping mechanisms that come with stress and endless pressure. The pressure of feeling disconnected from your loved ones and society, the pressure of family and friends who expect you to be happy and successful in your relationships, and the pressure of investing a lot of time and energy in your relationships without getting the results you want.

Self-love is where it all starts. If we want to have joyful work, decent co-workers, helpful managers, supportive friends, honest service providers, respectful strangers, loving neighbours, and a safer world to live in, that is free from emotional and physical hurt, crime, addiction and bullying, and full of happiness and peace, we must start with the family as the building block of society. Families start with couples, and to have happy couples we must start with healing the wounded selves first, letting them shine with love.

This book intends to touch hearts and attract open-minded people who value faith, hope and love in their lives. Establishing a healthy marriage, building a happy family, navigating the unknown, and overcoming tough times requires a strong belief that everything is solvable, which in turn generates hope to find the right solution. It also requires unconditional love, acceptance, and willingness to contribute equally to the success of relationships from all parties.

In this book, I teach you to fall in love with yourself so that you can extend this love to others. Your eyes will shine with happiness, and people will see beauty in your smile. Your soul will become ready to bond to your partner with love on all levels (emotional, mental, spiritual, and physical). Together, you will learn how to pass this tremendous love to your children – to raise them, hand-in-hand, while accepting their differences as new humans. You will be able to create the garden needed for your children to flourish and grow into the human beings they are meant to be.

Your children will drink the values of faith, hope, and love from you, and follow them throughout their lives. They will enter the external world full of confidence and ease in their own skin, creating peaceful connections with everyone around them. These children will grow to become our legacy on Earth, teaching and spreading love and peace all around them to the world. They will touch the hearts of people they come across, as I have touched the hearts of their parents, and they will become our messengers of love in every office, school, business, and home they visit. They will infuse happiness in all societies and create a happier world, as I do believe that "Happiness is the Legacy of Love".

For your children to develop into loving humans who spread peace and happiness to the world, we must work diligently in strengthening their self-worth which is the core of life. Self-worth is a common right for all humans, and it can only be cultivated with love. Ignoring this right is the same as saying "You don't have the right to live or exist on Earth". Such sentiments activate fear, which when suppressed, becomes magnified and pushes people to act mindlessly. That is why we need to give self-worth far more attention than it is currently given and treat it with tremendous respect.

We live in a blinded, traumatized world; a lot of emotional and physical hurt lies hidden under beautified words like *professionalism, official, formal,* etc. People forget a major aspect of human creation – emotions – and the unforeseen wounds created when emotions are treated as something unpleasant or undesired. All human beings possess the five birth right freedoms I mentioned a moment ago. When everyone equally practises these freedoms with the right support system, wisdom and tolerance, a lot of worldly suffering will disappear.

During my long journey of self-discovery, I took many accredited courses in coaching, NLP, hypnosis, and relationships. I read many books by different psychologists, and I kept pondering: why do humans do what they do? Why am I experiencing those hurts or setbacks? And how can I heal myself from my own wounds? I never hesitated to dig deeper into my inner world, which always helped me to elevate higher in my external one.

I also realized that what we need in life is to take great care of our free spirit, dissolving all constraints, self-rejection, and disbelief to grow limitlessly and shine our beauty to the world. From this, all possibilities begin. And what was once unimaginable becomes a tangible reality...

We will travel together in a journey to heal your deepest wounds and help you rewrite your story to be a joyful one. We will first tap into your courage, go through all the layers of darkness, find your inner gem and let it shine brilliantly. After that we will create a strong channel that connects you to the self and helps you fall in love with it head over heels. Once this unconditional love is established, you are guided to create the kind of life that you always wanted, by reclaiming your hobbies or initiating new interests. You will be able to understand when you are exercising love towards yourself and when are you deceiving it. And then you'll be ready to bridge with love towards another human being.

When two ready souls meet, they bond with love and do whatever it takes to sustain it and flourish it. As they tango with love, the resulting seeds will see, hear, learn, and touch the love around them. At that moment the dynamic expands, and we move from couples to families, and from families to societies, which aggregate together cohesively for a much happier world.

While helping many clients, and reading a lot about human psychology, I worked relentlessly to understand what people might be doing unconsciously in their relationships. This allows me to provide you with a logical and in many cases scientifically proven reason for it. I have been through pain myself; that has intrigued me to look for solutions. I have tried many that did not sustain until I reached a more consistent path, which I want to take you along while reading this book.

You may be a parent struggling with your teenager's behaviour, feeling stressed and wanting to find a solution; or a worker feeling overwhelmed due to co-workers' or manager's actions, which in turn affects your relationships with your beloved, and want to feel calmer and happier. You may be a couple arguing about little things leading to bigger conflicts and want to rekindle your love; or a daughter/son who wants to have a more harmonious relationship with your parents. You may be in a family suffering from lack of appreciation and cohesion between its members, and you need to strengthen your relationships' bonds; or a friend looking for stronger friendships with your peers. You may be a human craving to love yourself more. If so, you have landed at the perfect station.

From this station you will travel on the vehicle of your choice to the land of your dreams. There you will be introduced to the experiences of real people and get one-of-a-kind insights from their lives, which will make your heart sing with hope, love and joy. You will know that love is still there, inside all of us, and no matter what we have gone through, as humans we still have the capacity to love and be loved in the way we aspire to. And as others have experienced this kind of love, fulfilment, and joy in their lives, so can you. We all can have it with the grace of GOD.

But I have to warn you, if you are someone who gives up easily on yourself, someone unwilling to look bad before perfecting your relationships, if you are not willing to endure pain in order to heal and prefer to live your life pretending that all is well despite your deepest despair, then it is better to save your money and time. And if you are currently suffering from deep depression, reading this book will be nice, but you must look for professional help while going through the exercises, as you will need a lot of support along the way.

I advise you to read the book and do all the exercises in order, as each step leads to the next. I also encourage you to ponder for some time on the information and insights from each chapter before rushing to the next. Let's begin the journey towards more peaceful relationships, with yourself and others, cultivated through a healed past, self-acceptance, and unconditional love, for a happier and more peaceful world.

SECTION I

Our Wordly Mission

Our Pursuit of Worldly Love & Peace

Love turns wars into peace, conflicts into opportunities, diversity into strength, and can create a happier world by building happier families, one family system at a time.

> *"The day the power of love overrules the love of power, the world will know peace."*

— Mahatma Gandhi

I used to be a calm and introverted person, spending my time studying and reading, even during holidays. Whenever I attempted to blend with people, I would get hurt easily without being able to express my feelings or ask for things I wanted. Even when I tried to express my feelings, I did so to the wrong people who made me feel rejected, sad and miserable. I did not know how to belong or connect. I ended up hiding from the harsh outside world and suppressing my feelings, causing me to have health issues, lose opportunities, and feel lonely and disconnected.

While working in the corporate world, I also noticed how people were unloving towards each other, everyone living in an isolated land centred around themselves and their own needs, not caring much about other people's needs or how they feel. It seemed like a race; everyone was trying to win even if their winning meant harming others by words and actions. As love and peace are the top values in my life, I felt intrigued by these actions. I kept wondering how we can develop a more peaceful and happier world, by cultivating love and care between people, a world where we are happy and everyone around us is happy too.

By that time, I had two questions to answer: how can I fit in with the world without being hurt? And how can we create a more loving and peaceful world to live in? Several years ago, I saw my sister reading a book about relationships. I felt curious, so I bought it; then I bought and read many other books and took several courses by different psychologists and thought leaders. I also tried many healing modalities and was coached by different coaches for several years. All of them were great, and they brought amazing results, but their effect lasted only a short time; every time I would go back to my previous state and start taking a new course, reading another book, doing new healing. I felt confused and started thinking: why do such programs and healings work with other people but not me? What can bring me lasting change?

I was stuck in that cycle for many years until, in December 2019, I came across the Virginia Satir coaching and mentoring program created by Sharon Loeschen. Virginia was a pioneer family therapist who created the magical Change Process Model more than 30 years ago. Her model continues to be used by change managers and organizational gurus to define how change can impact organizations.

In the program, we study several models, concepts and tools. We have to go through extensive work on ourselves to enrich our relationships both with self and others, which is done under the supervision of a mentor before we can work with clients. I was lucky to have Aznive as my mentor, because she taught me the true meaning of self-acceptance despite weaknesses, mistakes, past experiences and pain; she taught the need for being congruent in expressing our feelings no matter what.

When I learned about the five human right freedoms that Virginia Satir identified (the freedom to see and hear what is going on here and now, rather than what should be, was or will be; the freedom to feel our feelings rather than what we ought to; the freedom to express our thoughts and feelings as they are; the freedom to ask for what we want without having to wait for permission; and the freedom to take risks on our own behalf rather than choosing to stay secure and not rocking the boat), understood the true meaning of self-love as being worthy to exist and have a place on earth, and learned about the concept of human parts, how every part plays a vital role in our lives, and how all members of a system influence its whole dynamic, everything started falling into place.

It only took a single human to touch my heart with love and help me to feel secure from rejection regardless of what happens and show me that I am worthy of love for who I am – not for what I achieve in life, what certificates or knowledge I have, or what position I hold or belongings I possess, regardless of my mistakes or what hurdles I have overcome.

This human was my mentor Aznive, and these are the things I learned to give others at Virginia Satir Global Network:

unconditional love and acceptance – bearing in mind that, as humans, we all need healthy physical, mental, emotional, and energetical boundaries for our total wellbeing.

That was the time when pivotal shifts started happening in my inner world and gradually manifested in my outer world through new decisions and actions. I was heard and seen as a human and became an advocate to deliver the message of love and peace of Virginia Satir, Dr Barbra De Angelis, and earlier our prophet Mohamed – Peace be upon him – who are my greatest role models in the field of relationship coaching. I want to show you how to be, think, feel, express and receive freely all the love that you deserve to receive and give to others. To create a new world that is a better place to live in.

In my efforts to make this dream come true, I collected all the knowledge gained from years of studying, reading books, thinking, analysing, researching, digging deeper and working with many clients, colleagues and acquaintances who got amazing results. I interviewed people who are currently living the dream and realized that in order to create a happy cohesive and peaceful world, we need to build happier more cohesive and peaceful families, one family system at a time. These families are the building blocks of societies, and from them we will get healthy happy souls, who will contribute to building a happier world.

To prepare these souls, our love ambassadors, at an early stage, I decided to work with them before they are born! This means before their parents get together to create the bond of marriage, resulting in conception and their birth on earth. The way to do this is to work with every individual to release their old baggage of hurt, shame, guilt, anger, and all limiting beliefs, to help them build an independent life that they love. Next is to work on their bonds of love and all the dynamics around it, before they can pass the mixture of unhealthy emotions to their children, and eventually to their grandchildren, and beyond.

This book will take you through a rebirth process. It has been structured sequentially, so make sure you go through all chapters and do all exercises in sequence to see how love transforms people into happier souls. This happiness shines from inside and is seen through the bright look in their eyes and their authentic smiles, creating an irresistible beauty on the outside. Are you ready to embark on this journey of love and peace? Let's begin.

SECTION 2

The Big Picture

The Magical Wand of Love

*Love is the hidden driving force that once activated,
will make humanity blossom.*

*"Love is the magician of the universe.
It creates everything out of nothing."*

— Dr Barbra De Angelis

*L*ove is the magic wand that, when it touches anything and everything, creates wonders. With love the ugly becomes beautiful, the bad becomes good, small things grow and flourish, and big things shine and magnify. It is love that makes the dead alive. It is the hidden force that once activated can move mountains and help us achieve the unexpected. It directs everything in our lives without us even realizing it. We go to places we love, practise the sports and hobbies we love, prefer to do work activities that we love, and spend time with people we love – all while being in the flow, with happiness and joy, losing any sense of time.

By the end of this chapter, you will be holding your breath from excitement and glee, as you discover the unspoken power of love. It is the power of ending wars and spreading peace in the world. "How is this?" you may ask with dismay. "Are you telling me that just love alone can end wars?!" My answer to you with unwavering confidence is: Yes, true love can prevent wars from happening in the first place. Throughout these pages you will learn the secret formula of this antidote, and how to put it into practise. You will learn how to cultivate it and get more of it in your life and the lives of your children, so that together we can build a much happier and more peaceful world.

You will find out that a loving mind is not a frightened mind; it does not tend to start a war of any kind, as it comes from a deep place of inner peace, safety and serenity. True love does not hurt, because its essence is light. It is rather fear that makes people invade each other, igniting flames of wars – inner wars within humans and outer wars between humans – causing them to attack and hurt each other to protect their fearful selves.

By studying and reading about human psychology and relationships, I came to understand what people do, both consciously and unconsciously, that affects their relationships with others and their whole lives. I realized how people in our societies are love deprived. Everyone is craving more love and acceptance; they want to make sure they are good or important enough to be worthy of love, and they are constantly seeking to be in the state of love, whether by reading about it, watching it, or listening to the stories of other people living it. They want to see evidence that it exists, and they can have it in their own lives.

What is interesting is that they don't confess this deeply hidden desire, or maybe they are not aware of it. People don't realize that in order to get love, they need to start a journey towards falling in love with themselves first, with all their parts, the good ones and the ones they consider not so good, the parts they feel proud of, and the ones they would rather hide. These parts can be thoughts, beliefs, emotions, or even physical aspects of self. Only when they love themselves will they be ready to connect to another human being with love and accept all their parts and aspects of self too.

You will be amazed to see how simple the process is if you have an open mind and heart to accepting and implementing it slowly but steadily, with strong faith and patience. This is my gift to you in these pages. I am sharing concepts about human love and relationships, followed by valuable tools and exercises that have worked with many people, including myself. You will find in each chapter real stories about people I have interviewed, who were generous to share a significant part of their lives to infuse hope and enlighten others. I have included the first and the last names of those who were willing to share them. For those who preferred to stay anonymous, I included a different first name only.

The Devastating Love Deficiency

I read a story in the newspaper several years ago about a man who had a conflict with his sister when she told him sarcastically "You are not laughing from the heart! Your laughter is fake!". They argued about this little thing a lot until it grew into something bigger and the brother harmed his sister. It happened when he felt deeply rejected and gave his power away to his supressed anger, allowing it at that moment to dominate his whole being. His unconscious behaviour drove him to do something that he is not so proud of. But this is how harmful craving for love and acceptance can be when not dealt with in a healthy way. What could have helped instead if the sister told him that she loved him, and she only thinks that if he laughed differently it would be more genuine. And from his end, he could simply explain that he feels rejected and thinks that she hates him from what she said. It is the lack of awareness in those moments that cause people to cope in unhealthy ways.

A client came to me feeling unbalanced and confused, with very low self-esteem. We kept exploring until we unravelled an old trauma of lost love in his life. His father had died when he was a teenager, causing him to develop unhealthy attachments to every person or thing he cares about. He was consistently anxious about losing his mother's love if she were to die too. When I worked with him on the traumatized part, the imbalance and confusion started easing for him. Only then could we start focusing on his goals in life and help him to move forward.

The Reviving Love

Once I read a remarkable story about how love turns the impossible into a miracle. In 1913, an American father from Virginia got a son who was born with no ears. When the doctor announced that the son would be deaf for his entire life, the loving father refused to accept this opinion as a fact, and he secretly declared in his heart that no matter what, his son would hear and speak.

He wasn't sure how, but with a strong faith, he did not doubt for a second that he would find a way to make it happen.

He decided to implant the desire to find ways to hear without the aid of ears in his son's mind, so that the son himself could translate this desire into tangible reality, and he did. As the child grew, his parents noticed that he could hear some sounds slightly, even though he still wasn't able to speak. That by itself was a great improvement, and it ignited the father's desire to wish for more, as he believed that what we can have some of, we can certainly magnify. And it again happened.

When the parents bought a victrola (a device for playing records), the child would react enthusiastically to certain songs, and keep playing them for almost two hours. He used to clamp his teeth at the edge of the case, allowing him to hear the sounds through bone conduction phenomena! Isn't this a way that his mind developed to hear sounds as a response to the desire of his loving father?!

Sometime later, the boy could hear his father clearly when words were spoken close to his skull at the base of the brain. He could even speak some words. The loving father wasn't tired or satisfied; he wanted more for his son, so he developed stories that he would tell his son during bedtime to induce his imagination to find ways to hear and speak clearly. He also wanted to convince him to treat his adversity as an asset of great value, even though he had no idea how.

The father started telling his son the incentives he would get due to his disability, like being treated with extra kindness by his teachers, which always happened, or that when he grew up and started his business of selling newspapers, people would give him extra money when they saw his intelligence, despite not having ears. These stories not only improved his son's hearing ability tremendously, but they also eliminated the slightest tendency of self-judgment or doubts due to his deficiency.

At the age of seven he sold his first newspaper, after borrowing six cents from a neighbour's shop without telling his parents. He kept selling and reinvesting the whole day, until he returned the money he borrowed and made a profit of 42 cents, which was a lot of money for a child at that time. What encouraged the little boy to do this do you think? It was his father's love, which turned into a firm sense of self-value and self-love. And it didn't stop there.

When the little boy grew, he went to high school and attended college, and even though he could not clearly hear his teachers unless they shouted from a short distance, he still made it without having to enrol at a deaf children's school. His parents didn't allow him to learn sign language and insisted that he associate with hearing children.

When he was at high school, he tried an electric hearing device and it wasn't helpful for him, but during his last year in college he got another device from a manufacturer as a trial, and when he tried it, he could hear everything clearly, like someone with ears! He could hear his mom, the radio and his schoolteachers so vividly! He could converse with people fluently! the miracle of love became true!

Then came the time to turn his handicap into an asset! The boy wrote a letter to the manufacturer describing his experience with an obvious sense of joy. They invited him to visit them in New York. While he was explaining what happened to the chief engineer in the factory, an idea came to his mind, that if he shares his story with the deaf people around the world, and told them about the new device, he could impact thousands of lives. He conducted market research, put a two-year plan to implement the idea and got a job with the manufacturer to make it happen by himself.

From then on, he devoted his life to helping people with hearing disabilities! How do you think this shift happened? It was due to his father's unconditional love, which translated into a high sense of self-worth and confidence to change his life, and then pour his love towards others as he made an impact on the world!

This is a preview of the chapters to come. It will help you understand the concepts covered in the book, and the sequence in which they are built.

Chapter 1: Falling In Love With Yourself

Looking to get love from others before giving it to the self will cause love to become a fable. No one will feed us portions of love. I wish such a thing existed. We need to cultivate self-love, feel complete on our own and develop an enriched relationship with ourselves first, before asking others to love us or being able to develop an enriched relationship with them.

The first step to reach there is healing the old wounds, as they obstruct awareness to inner resources and self-connection, impacting a person's self-esteem and sense of worth. Once this trauma is healed by loving and accepting all your parts, the physical parts and the intangible ones, the parts you like and the parts you dislike or hide, the beautiful parts, and the so-called ugly parts, the parts that play with you from day to day, and the ones you may be keeping in the shadow, you will get unstuck, and release all limitations and self-rejection. You will have an enriched relationship with yourself, build high confidence and approach life with a great sense of freedom.

This needs to be done with full compassion, even towards the parts of guilt, shame and self-blame. You need to assure them that it is ok to make mistakes, as the more we evolve in life, the better decisions we take. Accepting the message that each part is sending to us with love, learning the lessons that are meant be learnt in our life journey, and getting charmed by our inner world, will magnificently work to create for us the outer world we aspire. Doing this will develop inner peace and serenity from the inside that shines on the outside.

I will share with you the story of an exceptional lady who built a happy life through self-love, who contributed massively to the world not only by raising happy kids, but also by fostering and adopting many more, providing them with the same love and care she gave to her biological kids.

Chapter 2: Surviving Loss

Life happens! Even in the best situations a separation can take place due to death or divorce. I know death is tough; and I will do my best to tackle this overly sensitive topic with love and compassion, providing my distant support to help you mourn without sinking into your grief for the rest of your life. It is not healthy for you. The change that takes place with death is a fact of life that we cannot reverse by blaming ourselves or others, however difficult it is. And my heart goes to whoever is reading these words while being in the process of grief.

You will learn in this chapter that working on a relationship from one side for a long time can be exhausting, especially when the other person is so resistant to change. In these cases, you will need to make a decision and move forward. I love to say that "a healthy divorce is better than a dysfunctional marriage," for the sake of everyone, including children if there are any.

We sometimes see two good people on their own, but when it comes to building a healthy relationship between them, unfortunately, they don't have the ability to work on it together. Yes, I can help them, but only with their mutual consent and openness to work on the relationship together. If they are not willing to collaborate, at some point it may be better to just let go of it and move on.

I will take you through the stages of change to help cope with it in healthy ways. You will find me at your back, patting your shoulder to support you to continue your life, helping you to deal with those obstacles with an open mind and hurt to sustain hope while moving forward.

At the end of this chapter, you will find two stories. One is about a magnificent lady who mourned two amazing husbands and turned to uniting couples with love through her work. The second story is about a person who turned from divorce and the loss of almost every single asset he had to become a famous international photographer.

Chapter 3: Roadmap To Self-Love

After developing a powerful connection with yourself, you'll learn about different forms of self-love. Perhaps many people

Love Legacy

have told you to love yourself but without telling you how. You will find the answer to that question in this book. I'll also explain some love misconceptions in which people fool themselves into thinking that they love themselves, when in fact they are far away from self-love, leading them to cover it with unhealthy patterns.

I'll invite you to reclaim your childhood passions and lost dreams (i.e., hobbies, sports, interests, and things you find significant in life) by cultivating your love towards them and practising them more, to live a much happier and more peaceful life. During the process you may discover a hidden or secret passion that you were not aware of. As you start the self-exploration journey, like a new-born baby, you develop a creative ability to discover new things through your cultivated awareness. At the end of the chapter, I'll share with you the story of a lady who discovered a new passion she wasn't aware of, and it changed her life wonderfully.

Chapter 4: Bridging With Love

After building a happy and independent life centred around love and peace, you can develop a healthy and peaceful connection to another human being. Before doing so, you will need to understand how the world is living in excessive separation, not only physically, but also mentally and spiritually due to fearing each other. Reclaiming our five freedoms will be the solution that allows us to regain our original congruent self and present it to the world freely.

I'll take you through the process of dealing with differences in thoughts, opinions, and interests, accepting people for who they are without judgment, and pouring love from your cup into theirs. In this process you will need to work on building bridges of communication with respect and full acceptance to differences, shifting your focus from the self to the relationships you are creating with other people.

You will get to know how to deal with inevitable conflicts, considering them as an opportunity for growth, rather than being bad things to be avoided. This will help you to overcome tough times in your relationships, by activating your love gauge and consistently taking loving actions. I'll share with you an amazing story of a girl who took herself from being suicidal to becoming a successful human being. The power of a kind and loving connection with another special soul helped her to heal completely.

Chapter 5: The Happy Couple

When you get used to developing healthy, peaceful and happy relationships with friends, acquaintances and people in general, having a happy and healthy intimate relationship will become your new norm. You will be ready to invite the right soulmate into your life. The criteria of selection will differ from one person to another, based on what is important to them in a relationship. That's why building your own relationship vision board will be your reference for selection, considering that you need to be a ready soul first, in order to meet another ready soul.

You will learn how to send and receive love freely, mastering your language of love to fill your emotional tank and the tank of your beloved consistently. We'll look at one of the most damaging attachment styles in relationships, one in which people develop unhealthy coping mechanisms to deal with their lack of self-love while connecting to their partners. Being too dependent on their partners to give them love causes them to get stuck in an addictive relationships cycle. I refer to this attachment style as the narcissistic-co-dependence death dance. You will learn how to set yourself free from such an unhealthy pattern and start to tango with love.

You will learn how to ride the horse of your relationship without breaking it, by avoiding the four toxic behaviours of blaming, defending, stonewalling and contempt. You will know how to point out these toxic behaviours, and handle them wisely, whether you are the one who is practising them with your partner unconsciously, or you are on the receiving end as your partner uses them on you. I'll share with you two astonishing love stories allowing you to see how people apply love practically through their actions towards their beloved, keeping their relationships revived despite any obstacles.

Chapter 6: Building A Happy Family

Once you create a loving intimate relationship with a strong foundation, you will be ready to form a healthy and happy family. You will learn about the importance of building healthy boundaries between your newly formed family system and extended family and friends, for yourself, your spouse and your children. And you'll start making decisions based on what works best for your new system, not based on what works for others.

You will see how important it is to provide your kids with an environment that helps them grow and flourish, by teaching them how to love and be loved, through transferring your love to them, accepting their difference from you, from their siblings, and other kids too. Allow them to be the kind of human beings they are meant to be. You will see that raising kids is not much different from planting a seed and watching it grow with love and care.

You will learn about systemic roles and responsibilities, the importance of making them clear, and being open and willing to rotate them between family members. It is important to do this to avoid depressing situations resulting from holding a certain role for a long time. You need to unify the efforts of all family members to shift the focus on relationships rather than individuals.

I will introduce you to family dynamics, how the system's needs are voiced through its members, and how some roles arise in the system in order to regain its balance and reach its equilibrium. It is amazing how the family system speaks for itself throughout its members' behaviours, even when they do their best to hide or suppress them.

I'll tackle life shifts and turning points, and how we need to accept them rather than resist or deny them, to allow our minds to think about resilient solutions. This will allow you to send ambassadors of love and peace to the world, who will be able to connect with others to form healthy and happy relationships and contribute to building a happier world. I'll share with you the stories of two happy families of great couples who provided the right garden for their kids to flourish and grow into happy and loving contributors to the world.

Chapter 7: Creating A Happier World

Once we develop self-love as individuals, allowing us to connect with love to other human beings, create an intimate loving relationship with a soulmate, and build a happy and healthy family, we can start infusing love, understanding and acceptance at the workplace and other social settings for a happier society. You will learn in this book how to do this and more.

You will know how we are living in a traumatized world, due to collective pain and suffering. How small hurts can become deeper wounds, when not given the attention they require. How suppressed emotions get escalated, creating wars between people. You will know what happens when different systems collide and what can be done to deal with tough situations. You will learn how extensive efforts can heal people from the core, preparing societies to become vital bricks to building the happier world we envision.

Throughout the coming chapters, you will be introduced to a rebirth process that helps people to cultivate their inner peace, through developing unconditional love towards themselves and eventually to others. As love transforms people into happy souls, this happiness shines from inside and is seen through the bright look in their eyes and authentic smiles, creating an irresistible beauty that vibrates on the outside. And when a beautiful happy soul connects to another beautiful happy soul, we can only see more happiness and beauty in the world.

Can you see now how a lost love devastates and a living love revives? Which do you prefer? Waiting until the wound is created, gets deeper and hurts to start working on healing it? Leaving things as they are until wars destroy our lives? Feeling the deep pain before starting to think about how to fix it?! While this may be possible, in severe cases it will require a lot of effort and time. I invite you to become a strong believer in love as I am. This will be our pain prevention formula, and as we all know, prevention is always better than cure.

SECTION 3

Becoming a Ready Partner

CHAPTER 1

Falling in Love with Yourself

When you become at peace with the past, develop serenity from the inside out, and accept all your parts, you are on your way to a loving and happy relationship with yourself and others.

"If you don't love yourself, nobody will, not only that, you won't be good at loving anyone else. Loving starts with the self."

— WAYNE DYER

I cannot emphasize this enough. From my own experience and by observing others, I can say with unwavering confidence that what we have inside is what we manifest on the outside. If we love all of our parts and feel okay about them, then people will accept and feel okay about them too. The moment we start rejecting or resisting something in ourselves, we meet people who will remind us of this facet by rejecting it with us, sometimes in a cruel way, until we decide to wake up and make a different choice.

Oftentimes, people struggle to find the kind of love they want. But what if, in order to experience the love you aspire, you need to cultivate love and acceptance towards yourself before asking to receive it from others? We all have the right as well as the need to love and be loved, just the way we are. To achieve what we aspire to, it's crucial to define those needs and why they are important to us. How do we know we are loved? What does love mean to us? When do we live in a state of love? What does a loving, happy and healthy relationship with ourselves look like?

Once we develop a crystal-clear image of how to live in this state of love, we start taking conscious decisions about how to make this happen. It might occur through our actions towards ourselves, through the people we invite into our lives, jobs, hobbies or the tasks we engage in; they will be the foundation of building an enriched relationship with the self and others. By the end of this chapter, you will have a clear image of how to love yourself in a way that allows you to invite only love to your life and become ready to build healthy and happy relationships with others.

Have you ever thought to yourself "I wonder why people are mean to me? Why do they keep criticizing me? Or not give me what I deserve?" If this is your inner talk, then let me tell you that you are not alone. I have been there too! I had an unhappy career life. I felt stuck and was not able to move further despite all the efforts I put in.

I would not dare to ask for a promotion. I always treated people as though I was grateful, they were giving me the chance to exist in the world, by talking to me, giving me attention, or becoming my friends. Some of those friendships were emotionally and mentally abusive or toxic. It did not matter. What mattered the most was to say that I had friends, or at least people who were willing to let me call them my friends.

Why do you think this was happening? It took me a long time to realize that I had an extremely low self-image. It wasn't until I studied the Virginia Satir coaching and mentoring program that I came to know I was rejecting many parts of my being as a human. I have dived into my soul, reached levels I never expected to reach, and learned to accept myself and appreciate it first. I realized that tolerating bad behaviours from others was a result of thinking "Maybe this is what I deserve to get. The crumb". The good news is I am not there anymore, and I don't want this for you either.

The moment I started accepting all my parts, even the upset, angry, blaming, and criticizing ones, my life started changing gradually. I stopped tolerating bad behaviours from others and started expressing this easily and congruently. I started eliminating what was not serving me in life and cleared the space for much better people to come into it. If you relate to my story, then let me tell you that your worth is much higher than you think, and you deserve more than you are getting now. You need to first believe it and become at peace with who you are as a human by falling in love with yourself first.

The myth of love

Some people may say: "love is a miracle that requires an extraordinary power to happen, and only a few people in life experience it". I used to think this way before. Now I believe that love is within all of us, and we only need to be willing to tune into it and activate it in our whole life. It is also everywhere around us. To receive it we need to open up to the possibility that it exists, and that we can have it any time we wish to. Only then we can live in the state of love in our bodies' sensations and mental thoughts. As we open up our hearts, and listen to our needs, we allow ourselves to clear our energy channels to send and receive love easily and fluently. Love is an e-motion (an electrical signal produced by stimuli that gets in motion inside our bodies), that charges us with energy all the time.

Our capacity to love and accept ourselves reflects how much we can give love to and receive it from others. Dr Angelis once said: "All our relationships are our mirrors, and all people are our teachers", so if we treat ourselves with nobility and care, we will be able to treat others this way, and others will treat us in the same way.

Healing old wounds

"Is my past illuminating my present or contaminating it?"

— VIRGINIA SATIR

If love is ubiquitous, what do you think stops us from experiencing it consistently? It is the accumulated wounds and unpleasant experiences that clog this energy channel. These old wounds are often called "traumas". To clear our love energy channels, we need to heal those traumas delicately, with empathy and compassion. Regardless of their root cause – whether they came from surviving a war or natural disaster; experiencing violence or abuse, acute accidents, severe illness, post-surgery pain; or undergoing persistent stressful situations – their adverse effect on human psychology is the same. All of us are prone to it, both as children and adults, especially when our world becomes highly unpredictable.

Inner wounds create heavy weights on our shoulders, not allowing us to live our lives fully with ease. They blur our vision and don't allow us to see either the beauty in our lives or the bad situations calling for our attention to do something. Traumas keep us scared of what could happen, hindering us from moving forward. We become like war survivors, who even after their physical injuries are healed, their souls remain wounded. Every unexpected situation or less-than-kind word pushes us into excessive pain and suffering.

Once traumas are healed, they bring huge transformation to a human on all levels (psychological, spiritual, mental, physical, and social). It is the responsibility of every individual, community and society to handle trauma with love, acceptance and enormous kindness.

Another critical adverse effect of trauma is wanting for others what we want for ourselves. If a person is unconsciously practising unloving actions towards him or herself, like living repeatedly in an unhappy old story, that is the form of love s/he knows and will want for others. By doing so, the world lives in unconscious chaos due to an insufficient definition of love. Traumas become the basis of our decisions on how to think, what to feel, what actions to take; they become the steering wheel of our whole lives. The question is, do we really need to carry this heavy burden for the rest of our lives? I doubt it.

Deeply wounded people will bring more suffering to themselves and others because pain is the only response they have learned. In order to change, new information is needed. The process of healing starts when wounded people decide to step back from their stored memories and free themselves and others from comparison or blame; when they bring more compassion to their lives, get exposed to happier experiences, and approach life with tremendous curiosity; and when they release judgment and start implementing the new information consistently until they develop a new happy and peaceful state of being. Only then we can say that they are healed and will be able to bring more love to themselves and others.

Dr Peter A. Levin proposes important aspects to be considered while treating trauma. He mentions that we need to understand the complex connection between our bodies and minds, how they communicate through several pathways, and how they are affecting each other. He says that each organ of the body has thoughts, feelings and triggers attached to it, and is able to communicate with and listen to other organs too. The conventional way of dealing with trauma is by talking to vent out and by using chemical medication. That by itself is not enough to heal. It only suppresses the symptoms without tackling the root cause of it. It will be more efficient to follow a psycho-somatic approach where the body's intelligence is utilized to heal it.

Dr Navana Kundu said "There is no way you can release your past baggage and say that is it! I am done! Because baggage will keep being formed as we go through life. We need to consistently deal with them, to learn the lessons they hold for us". This means that you will need to deal with your daily issues, thoughts and emotions as long as you are breathing, and your heart is beating with life.

Trauma is defined as a painful experience that is formed by the way the mind processes information received. When infants receive information from their surroundings, through the five senses, this information gets recorded in the mind as memory. When this information is associated with pain, a belief is formed around it as something unwanted or a threat. After that, these beliefs get reinforced by living similar painful experiences through different scenarios, and they become stronger and deeper.

The person grows and goes through life, while information continues being gathered through the five senses. But now it gets filtered by the previously formed beliefs before being recorded in the memory. It conforms with the previously stored experience that is linked with pain, and triggers emotions associated with it, causing the person to unconsciously react to it and suffer. People start interpreting life events, situations they live, and other people's actions through a narrow lens called perspective, which is based on their formed beliefs, and a natural dependence on one sensory system over others. For example, some people may notice the colours and scenes of an experience vividly, while others store sounds associated with it and don't remember the visuals.

People are so identified with thoughts and emotions generated based on their perceptions. They build their whole life around them. However, these perspectives are incomplete. When people draw conclusions based on these perspectives, their judgement may not be accurate or true. Because the angle they are looking through could be a single situation or limited amount of information. By doing this, they restrict themselves from experiencing life and limit their options. As the mind continues collecting and recording information uncontrollably through life, this loop of suffering will continue, until it is healed by some kind of intervention.

When people decide to detach themselves from the experience and stop defining themselves by it, their traumas start to resolve. They can also prevent new traumas from happening by treating painful experiences as something happening around them, not *to* them, and they are doing their best to deal with, without allowing it to dictate how they feel. Something important needs to be said here: I don't mean that when you go through a painful experience you should not feel pain, or when you see a scary scene you should not feel scared. I rather mean to say that you can stop allowing this kind of feeling to dominate your life. Every human being, regardless of the hurdles they went through, has the capacity to do this and heal themselves.

Healing is a rebirth process, where transformation starts from within. With time, and consistency in applying it, change starts manifesting in the physical realm. This requires going through the following stages:

Rebirth Stages

Stage 1: Realization

Realization of the problem is the first step of healing it. That's when it is moved from our subconscious mind to the conscious mind, and we admit its existence.

Stage 2: Speaking up

Speaking up the problem is when we make a promise in front of others to heal ourselves. This will hold us accountable to keep the promise.

Stage 3: Taking action

Taking action is when the inner valve starts turning, and the shift begins to happen.

Stage 4: Dealing with resistance

Dealing with inner and outer resistance with gentle persistence shows yourself how much you love it, and how much you want the healing to happen.

Stage 5: Tangible changes

Noticing changes, accepting and appreciating them is the time when we start reaping results in the physical realm, as the new belief system starts forming.

Stage 6: Reinforcement

Tony Robins says, "Repetition is the mother of skill". In this stage you are going to repeat stage 5 until it becomes your new reality. With enough repetitions change becomes irreversible. As you are stacking on it more and more, it is pushed deeper and becomes the new norm.

Stage 7: Celebration

Celebrating your rebirth is like acknowledging your new reality; it is rewarding yourself for the hard work, recognizing that change has happened with no doubts, and welcoming the new you. This can be as important as all the previous stages. When people ignore it, they open themselves to thinking at some point that they still haven't healed. They trick their minds by jumping from one healing modality to another, while all they needed was just to stick with one of them long enough to reap results, trusting that change is happening, and the transformation process has already begun.

The Power of Acceptance

During the process of healing old wounds and cultivating self-love, it is important to develop unconditional acceptance for all aspects of life and self. When an event happens, or we go to certain places, meet particular people, or someone says something, our bodies may get triggered and respond with pain or uncomfortable sensations. In these cases, the body is alerting us about a condition that requires our attention. If this alert is ignored consistently, it causes chronic illness.

All emotions, like anger about the past, fear, sadness... etc., or aspects about self, like being moody, impulsive, needy, controlling or critical are called parts of self. These parts serve a purpose and come with a positive intention to help us cope with a situation, or to give us valuable information. If we choose to suppress and reject them, they only intensify, and with time manifest in the form of a chronic illness or pain. We may choose to reject this painful part again by ignoring or numbing it with painkillers, or we can choose to love it, giving it our attention, and exploring what is happening internally.

Let's say I experience certain pain; this pain is a manifestation of my body's voice calling for more care to be given to a particular organ, or to stop unhealthy food or habits. If I immediately take a painkiller without exploring the cause of pain, it is as if I am shutting off this voice and sending a message to my body that whatever is happening is insignificant. This will cause it to magnify and get louder until I listen to it. It may divert into a different form of distraction to get my attention, causing me to have negative thoughts and behaviours, like food addiction, spending a lot of time obsessing about a particular problem, watching TV for long hours.... etc. All of this will take me far away from my goals in life, leaving me unhappy. The body is so smart and will always find creative ways to tell us what is needed.

We need to be really careful here. If this is how we treat our inner voices, then we are stonewalling ourselves, which is a form of toxic behaviour that will bring into our lives people who will exercise it with us. Instead, we can ask ourselves "What is the positive intention of this part? What does it need?". If we cannot get satisfying answers by ourselves, then looking for help from a physician, or emotional, or spiritual guide is an option. Once we get more information, we shall start taking active steps towards satisfying these needs. Only then the pain will reduce and gradually disappear – when we treat it with love and acceptance.

When people believe in themselves, stop having the urge to convince others about their abilities or point of view, feel happy about the human being they are and don't seek people's approval, they become so joyful about their wholeness and holiness, as Virginia Satir describes. That's the kind of healthy relationship with the self we want to see. When a person is in full acceptance of his/her parts, it becomes like an invitation for others to accept this wonderful human being the way they are. At that moment they feel a great sense of freedom from the chains of other people's approval, and they become unstuck.

I once asked a client what he wanted to work on. He started talking about getting a better job opportunity. While stating all the reasons for not getting one, he said "I am also fat". Then he stopped talking for a few seconds before telling me that he had tried several diets, but nothing worked for him. His pause made me wonder "So, what if he is fat? Was he pausing to give me a chance to comment on it? As if I *must* say something about it or deny it? or is it so painful to him that he feels embarrassed to say it?".

Having some extra pounds and taking the necessary steps to reach the weight you want, for your own health, does not mean you need to stop living before reaching there. You can instead take determinant actions to reach where you want, while treating yourself with compassion and love. If you are rejecting a part of yourself (in this case it was the heavy weight) and not expecting to get a job before getting rid of that part, how will other people accept you and give you what you want?

Give yourself the permission to be who you are, the awesome human being called "you". Once this is done, your whole outlook will change and the responses you elicit in your life will become different. This happens when we become aware of our inner resources and the wholeness of our spirits. To reach this awareness we need to slow down and allow all the chaotic thoughts to pass by and go. This will allow us to reach our inner wisdom and find choices from an empowered state rather than a helpless one.

If we haven't practised enough self-love and care towards ourselves so far, it's okay. Even if our blaming part argues with us or points fingers, we can turn to it to calm it, appreciate the message it is carrying to us with love, and start practising the kind of self-love we want. Every single day is a new opportunity to do this. We will continue doing it for the rest of our lives. Remember that every moment is an opportunity to take a different choice. Let this choice be "The choice of love". Make a pledge to fall in love with the unknown parts of yourself, which carry great potential, but you may have not gotten the chance to access them yet.

Developing deep serenity

Ancient philosophers say that the spirit is not the mind, nor the body, nor the emotional state, nor the personality. And I cannot agree more with this, as the spirit or the soul is something mystical. It's something to be adored because it's what our creator blew in us to turn our dead bodies into living beings. He put in us holy characteristics, one of which is peace.

In my religion, we greet other people by saying "Peace be upon you". We also say it when enter an empty room, to start our existence in that place with peace.

If you ask me "What is the way to peace?". I'll say, "The shortest way to peace is love! more and more love". Love infuses peace and transforms people to bring them closer to their true spirit, the spirit they are meant to be, which worships GOD out of gratitude (not just fear), and builds earth with loving acts towards self, things, and others. I deeply believe that any hurdle in life can be overcome with more love and compassion, as the more love we have, the more peace we can spread to the world.

Once we comprehend this truth, taking it in with our whole being, we will become madly in love with ourselves, head over heels. Our inner peace and tranquillity will expand awareness about our true selves and open to us new possibilities. We are no longer helpless, hopeless or weak. Our inner fire ignites, and we feel that we can conquer the world, while we choose to do it with a loving peace and a peaceful love. There will be no loneliness anymore. No feeling of fear or sadness, because we know we are whole and connected to ourselves and our creator. We can easily and fluently expand this connection to others as we want and whenever we want.

You may wonder "How do I bring more love to myself or the situation?". This can be done by slowing down, being silent, watching your thoughts with respect, observing your body sensations, writing or drawing all thoughts and emotions on paper with relevance to the situation and other people, and then thinking about what can make you and others happy in the best way possible. The calmer you are, the more open you become to receiving valuable information about yourself and others, and the clearer the solution will be.

Tune into your mind, body, heart and spirit. Show them care and compassion every single day. This is how you can enrich your relationship with the person living with you now and for as long as you live. All relationships with others will flourish with love. A friend told me once "If you never make fresh juice for yourself, how can the person you marry expect that you love drinking fresh juices and make it for you sometimes? He'll never do it, because he will probably think that you don't like it, or don't consider it as a form of love, since you don't show it to yourself". We need to teach people how to love us, by showing them how we love ourselves and what makes us happy in life.

After developing a strong connection and understanding to yourself, you can create strong connections with others. These connections will come from a healthy and whole place, not from a needy place, where you look for someone else to fill the void in you. Only then can you connect without attachments to the results, or to how people will react. No matter what happens, you will see yourself as a complete person, fulfilling your needs from an endless inner source, that takes full responsibility for your peace, tranquillity and feelings of love.

This inner source becomes your fuel and a spark of happiness shines in your eyes. It is the anchoring source to navigate through life with an authentic smile, believing that all is well and is happening for the good. Self-esteem can get distorted by other people's opinions and external events, or even past experiences in which we couldn't achieve what we wanted. But when we become silent and tune into our true selves and endless resources rather than depending on people's opinions and outer world experiences, we can build a self-esteem immune to criticism. We stop being so cautious and dependent on other people's opinions about us to believe in what we can do.

There are two keys to building happy and healthy relationships with the self and others

Key 1: Be connected with the self, showing it much love, care, compassion and acceptance.

Key 2: Be honest about what is going on inside us, communicating it congruently without jeopardizing our self-esteem. If self-esteem is injured the connection is not based on self-love; and when there's a lack of self-love in the communication, it cannot be a loving one. The relationship then becomes unhealthy and consequently unhappy.

Exercise 1.1: I love myself game

A great tool to improve love towards self and others is the "I love myself game". I learned this tool from great teachers of love and relationships and added a few things to it. When I applied it continuously, my self-esteem was uplifted massively. And I am sure it will do wonders for your life over time.

1. If you prefer writing you can use the space after the exercise or assign a notebook for all the exercises in the book,

starting with this one. And if you prefer talking get an application on your phone where you can record messages and save your recordings.

2. Do it in the most comfortable way for you. If you love talking to yourself in the mirror, do it, if you prefer another way then follow the most convenient way for you.
3. Start with "I love you, (your name)", so if I am going to write this letter to myself in my notebook or record it, I would say "I love you, Reem".
4. Follow this with "I really, really love everything in you..." and start mentioning all your traits (physical, mental, spiritual, emotional, way of dealing with things, character, everything in you).
5. The second day open what you wrote or recorded and read it/listen to it. Make sure not to skip this.
6. Then tell yourself "Thank you (your name) for loving me, I accept it and appreciate it!".
7. You will eventually smile, and if not, try to wear a nice smile while saying it.
8. Do it even if you don't believe it. A new belief will be imprinted in your mind over time. The more you do it, the stronger and faster it will happen. Even in the moments I used to feel stressed, I would look in the mirror after brushing my teeth in the morning to affirm my self-love and acceptance, and it really helped me.

_____

_____

_____

_____

_____

_____

Exercise 1.2: Define your self-love map

In this exercise you will be able to define where you are in terms of self-love, where you want to reach, and how to close the gap in between. Take your time pondering each question and write whatever comes to your mind. You can come back later to refine it as many times as you want.

1. What does the word "love" mean to you?

_____

_____

2. What does self-love mean to you?

_____

_____

3. On a scale of (0-10) 0 being "I don't love myself at all" and 10 "I love myself a lot", how much do you think you love yourself?

_____

_____

4. On a scale of (0-10) how much do you want to love yourself?

_____

_____

_____

5. Why is self-love important to you?

_____

_____

6. Connect to your heart and answer this question: When your goal of self-love is achieved, what will happen in your life as a consequence?

_____

_____

7. How will this make you feel?

_____

_____

8. You can go as deep as you want by repeating questions 5–7 until you feel at your peak.
9. Now draw two circles like in the figure bellow and write in the first one "My current self-love status", with the score you

got for it from step 3. In the other circle write "My desired self-love status (goal)", with the number you got from step 4.

10. Write under the goal circle how your feelings will be and what changes will happen in your life when this goal is achieved (your why). Dream big and be honest with yourself on what you really want and what will happen.

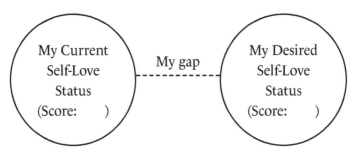

When I reach this goal, I will feel

_____

And these changes will happen in my life

_____

_____

11. Now ask yourself "What are the skills and capabilities you think you need to reach your goal?"

_____

Who can help you reach them?

_____

What are the resources you need?

_____

12. Be creative and limitless in expressing your deepest
    thoughts, feelings and desires.
13. Now think about the easiest and most appealing thing you
    can do as the first step towards achieving your goal. I am
    sure you have the answers, trust yourself in this, knowing
    that I trust you.

_____

Exercise 1.3: Accepting all your parts

This exercise will help you define the parts that you may be
unconsciously rejecting. It will also help you accept those parts,
learn the messages they are carrying with love, and make better
decisions – because you are moving towards more self-love and
self-acceptance in your life.

1. Find a quiet place away from distractions.
2. Sit comfortably and close your eyes.
3. Start inhaling and exhaling slowly and deeply.

4. Imagine a white light filling your head, neck, shoulders, spine, and all your organs.
5. Tell yourself "I Love Me".
6. Watch out for any objection from your body that comes in the form of pain or a voice in your head.
7. If this pain or voice had a shape, what would it look like? What colour does it have?
8. If you give it a name, what would it be?
9. Listen for the message it is carrying for you with love.
10. Start a conversation with this part and ask if something you do triggers it.
11. Acknowledge its feelings, assure it love and acceptance as it is part of you.
12. Thank it for the message and for serving you all the time before; apologize if you need to.
13. Then, instruct this part to trust you and give you the control as an adult who knows the best decision to take in different situations. Let it allow you to have a different choice for expressing your needs.
14. See if there are any changes to the initial shape, colour, voice...etc.
15. Ask this part to be with you in your heart along the journey, assuring it love and acceptance.
16. Take your time to process all this. Once you are ready, open your eyes.
17. Carry this new learning in your everyday life, and use it to grow wiser, happier and more loving to yourself.

Additional sources

♥ You can find an interesting article about accepting your parts on my website. It is called "Embracing your monster and choosing love".
https://www.reemahmed.life/embracing-your-monster-and-choosing-love/

♥ This healing meditation utilizing the power of infinite love and gratitude is amazing. I have done it myself and shared it with people. Everyone found it very useful, especially when done daily, for a long time (a month at least). https://youtu.be/hktYE2sWkE

I understand that social conditioning, subliminal brainwashing, physical constraints (including environmental circumstances and health issues) and energy vampires can be destructive to self-worth. But unless you decide and put effort into dealing with these love barriers, they will not dissolve by themselves, and you will remain stuck and unable to move anywhere. To get rid of these barriers you need to start watching your habitual thinking. Do you often think about what could go wrong? About how people will heart you? About the damage that could happen? These thoughts are usually associated with fear.

You need to understand the root cause of this pattern, either by reading and searching or by getting the help of an expert. Accept all your parts, even the ones that initially look ugly to you; they are there for a good reason, and to serve you when you decide to use them mindfully. Define your goals of self-love and take baby steps towards achieving them.

If you do all of this and still feel something is not going well, then maybe you need to explore some buried parts that want to come out. Seek their help, and work on activating them and bringing more of them to your day-to-day life. By doing this you will experience massive changes in your life.

But if you are scared to dive in and explore your unseen parts, to acknowledge that you have been rejecting them for so long – if you lack the courage to say "Sorry...Please forgive me...Thank you...and I love you..." to all your parts, then be ready to remain stuck and living an unfulfilled life.

When we adore the person we are, treat ourselves with love and compassion, and give ourselves the permission to make mistakes and learn from them, it becomes so easy to forgive ourselves, wipe out the painful experiences from our memories, develop inner peace and move forward. When we cultivate this amazing inner environment, we start seeing our endless resources and true potential for what they are, unbounded by people's limited opinions about us.

Accept, love and embrace your weak parts as much as you do to your strong parts in order to accelerate your healing process, then harness your strengths rather than focusing on what is missing in you. Stop punishing yourself for not being good at something, because it elicits low self-worth in you and that's not an act of love. Understand that when you improve your strong parts it's as if you are constantly giving yourself applause for being good at something, anything. This will elevate your self-worth tremendously.

Express your feelings once you feel them. Being okay with your self-expression, not feeling ashamed or having that weird sensation in your stomach or that choking in your throat while talking about them is a pure act of self-love. And if you feel guilt or blame, be mindful that some parts might be rejecting each other, which can happen. You need to be that maestro who masters the situation and loves them all equally. That's true self-love and acceptance. At the end of this chapter, I will share the story of a glorious woman in her seventies who teaches us the truth about love by example.

If you need help at any point, come back to this book, read it again, and remember that I am always here for you, to support you, encourage you, and cheer you up during your rebirth process. I'll always be by your side to tell you "Well done for paying attention to your inner world! Bravo for the courageous work you are doing! You are an amazing person with all your parts, and worthy of love".

After learning about the power of love, how it can help us in healing old wounds and allowing us to accept ourselves for who we are with all our parts, we are in a place where we can develop deep serenity from inside that radiates peace and beauty on the outside. But what if we are hit with new losses, creating new wounds in our lives that affect our core and leave us devastated and unable to move forward? How can we survive?

In the coming chapter you are going to learn about two of the most catastrophic types of personal crises, that can apprehend us from our lives and rob the power to move forward. These two crises are the death of a beloved and getting divorced. Don't panic. I will be there with you along the way through my words and soul. I assure you that I will do my best to support you as much as I can until you become a happy contributor in the world and send amazing souls to it.

Mama Gladys &
The Truth About Love

*"Goodbyes are only for those who love with their eyes.
Because for those who love with heart and soul there is
no such thing as separation."*

— RUMI

In my search for stories about a wondrous love for self and others, despite all the pitfalls, I came across the story of Mama Gladys. When Gladys met James, she was still living with her previous husband, but her relationship wasn't great. She was thinking about leaving town. At that time, she had two kids (Larry and Bill) and was pregnant with a third (my amazing and dear friend Thelisia). When James heard her story, he advised her not to leave and promised to help her as much as he could. James was also coming out of a marriage. And this is how their story started.

James was a butcher and security person at a grocery store near Gladys' house. In the beginning, they were only friends helping each other. Gladys felt something special towards him from the very first moment they met. He was sweet, talked nicely, acted with kindness, and was easy to talk to, which were very important qualities to her. He was very quiet and did not bother anybody, but people were scared of his serious character. Although he was quiet, when he spoke, he would have everyone's full attention.

Gladys and James were friends for 10 years before getting married. This allowed them to know almost every single detail about each other. He loved her kids a lot. He taught her how to fish with a rod and reel, and they used to spend a lot of time fishing together. James had four children from his previous marriage, and she supported and admired him a lot. With time, they fell in love. They decided to get married in 1983 and lived together after their wedding for 35 years, as he passed away in 2019.

In Gladys' opinion, it is important when meeting someone to talk to them openly and get to know them well before deciding whether to marry them. I am not saying you have to wait 10 years, as she did. But you need to give yourself a chance to know the person well. The way she/he treats you will mirror how much love you have for yourself at the moment and inform you how ready you are to receive love from others.

According to Gladys, it is crucial to ask the person you meet – and allow them to ask you – about the most important things in your life. Only in this way you can claim that you know them, and they know you. These questions could be something like:

- ♥ What does that person like?
- ♥ What do they want in life?
- ♥ What do they enjoy doing at the weekend?
- ♥ What do they expect from this relationship?
- ♥ What do they expect from you?
- ♥ Do they want kids?
- ♥ How do they treat their parents?

- How much respect do they have for their family?
- What are their values?
- What they don't value in life?
- What are their plans?
- How do they express their happiness, anger and sadness?
- Do they believe in budgeting and saving their money?
- Will they support, protect and defend you as much as they can, and whenever needed?

Our answers to such questions when asked must be honest. If we lie, we encourage the other person to lie to us. Just as important, we don't allow the other person to know us for who we are, and they will fall in love with someone we are pretending to be, not us. Gladys was sure to tell James the truth about her and he loved her anyway. In turn, she learned who he was and what he stood for.

Doing this allowed them to build a deeper connection. One time, James was taking Gladys somewhere without telling her where they were going. They had been driving for a while, and the atmosphere was so quiet. She turned to him to ask where they were going, and before she spoke, he said "Just sit down and relax, you will see when we get there". It was a movie in another city. It was good and she loved it. He knew what she liked without her even telling him, because he loved her so much and had paid attention. She showed him her true self, so his predictions were correct!

Total honesty is very important in relationships. But we cannot reach it unless we are in full acceptance of who we are in every single aspect of our lives. We must love ourselves unconditionally, living happily by ourselves without waiting for someone to come and MAKE us happy – because no matter what they do, we'll never feel happy unless we are happy from inside. Gladys adds that when a person is not totally honest, they will always have to hide something when things come up. But if they tell the truth about everything and the other person still likes them, then they have a shot at being very happy. That's what she and James did.

During their 35 years of marriage, Gladys and James took care of many kids. They had seven kids from their previous marriages (She had two boys and one girl, and James had four girls). They didn't have more biological kids after their marriage, but they adopted two kids who were developmentally delayed (Jonathan who was adopted when he was four years old; he is now 30, and Quanisha was adopted when she was three and is now 24). They also fostered many kids; she cannot remember how many. They were foster parents for five years and medical foster parents for 25 years, taking care of children with many types of disabilities.

They spent many years with so many kids in the system. Before she started fostering, people used to laugh about her lifestyle and call Gladys "The Salvation Army". Then, it became a formal way of living and helping others. After these kids would leave the system, they'd always go back to visit her again. When she used to go for picnics or other public places with her family, someone would call out "Mom!" and she would turn around without knowing who that was, because there had been so many of them. Her biological daughter Thelisia would say "You are not everybody's mom!". Then she would laugh and say: "I got used to sharing you anyway, so that's not a problem".

Gladys and James used to take each kid on an individual basis. Then they would try to understand where they came from and what it would take to reach them. Some were mentally impeded or had faced different kinds of abuse, but the kids trusted them and would share with them what they refused to share with their own therapists. There were always kids at her house who were from the neighbourhood. Her house was the home kids would flock to.

It was a joyful process because she loved kids and believes that they have a lot to say, but people hear them without listening to their yearnings. James was helping her a lot in taking care of those kids. They loved him and he would always listen to them. After James passed away, in the spring of 2019, Gladys turned 75 and started taking care of her 97-year-old mom. She had to stop fostering children because it was difficult without James.

The grandma had been living by herself until she was 96 in Ocala, the town where Gladys' older brother lived, in her spotless apartment. One day she fell and was no longer able to live alone. After about a year of being with Gladys, she had an infection in her lungs. They took her to the hospital where she was given antibiotics and her condition improved, but she became afraid to stand and walk by herself again. The grandma now is bedridden and living with Gladys in Miami, where she is getting physical therapy to regain her strength.

Gladys didn't have any dreams before getting married other than having a house full of kids. She thought of becoming a nurse, but she didn't. Ironically, this is what she ended up doing by fostering kids with medical conditions after marrying James. Besides that, she had a full-time job as a supervisor for the Data Processing Unit in the Health Department at the State of Florida. James was a very kind, patient and caring husband, who was willing to retire before her to take care of the kids. He attended special classes with her to become officially eligible as a medical fostering parent. James was always fair to her and to everyone, something she misses a lot now. If he said he would do something, she knew she could depend on him. She never had to remind him about something she had asked for, she would just ask and leave it, trusting that when he had time, she would surely get it.

Gladys had zero fears about the relationship. She never thought James would leave her because he was a keeper. He always said to people, and to her, that she was stuck with him. Both of them were happy with it. She got so comfortable in this relationship and expected everything to be the same always, but it wasn't. He passed away and she now misses him a lot. She is having many lonely days but thinks no one can replace James in her heart. She is satisfied for the time GOD gave her with this amazing husband. What a loving marriage story.

She didn't drive for many years; James would always take her wherever she wanted. He would wait for her in the car until she was ready, without being bothered by the heat. Sometimes she felt guilty and asked him to go inside instead of waiting outside in the car, but he would say "It is okay!". People watched this amazing couple without them knowing it.

Gladys knew that James was the one when she was feeling safe and happy with him. She didn't have to bother about anything. He was decent with the kids, and rather than just taking over the role of a father, he spoke to them, explained his new role and allowed them to ask any question they wanted.

They had a nice simple wedding. She bought her wedding gown from Sears Department Store for just $58. People thought it was her grandmother's dress, as it was so pretty on her and looked like an antique. Her best friend made the veil for her, which had the exact same lace as the dress! What a lovely coincidence. And her youngest son was the one who gave her away to the groom!

Gladys enjoyed fishing with her husband a lot. They spent their honeymoon fishing. I asked Gladys if she thought uncommon interests might impact a loving marriage. She said yes. If the husband is busy doing something all the time that his wife is not interested in, it might cause her to become miserable. Having common interests or developing and/or learning about things that your spouse loves will positively impact your relationship. To Gladys, sharing interests with James, like fishing and watching football games, was a fun process. It made it easier for them to be together all the time and played an important role in the success of their marriage.

Another aspect of a successful marriage is being able to talk about subjects that some couples find hard to even bring up. Gladys believes that love is truth. It is believing in and respecting the other person, knowing and trusting that they will always have your back, and will always be there for you. It is not in money and materialistic things. I love to say that trust and respect go hand-in-hand in relationships; if one of them is broken, the other is broken. When there is no respect, there is no love, and when there is no trust, there are a lot of fears. The feeling of safety is like a cornerstone in a relationship; it cannot be sustained without it.

Gladys also believes that when you respect the other person totally, there are boundaries that you don't cross. We need to do whatever it takes to maintain respect and keep the other person in a loving and secure place, otherwise love will gradually disappear. She saw some people being bullied into relationships, feeling like they must have someone to help them raise their kids, as if they could not manage without the other person. Gladys thinks that is not true.

Gladys adds that it is important not to allow anybody to say something negative about our beloved. If we are having negative thoughts due to something that happened between us and our partners, that's okay. We can talk to them about it with total honesty. But these thoughts shouldn't come from anyone else. We must close our ears to them. She believes that some people are jealous or envious and they will not want us to be happy. They might be doing it consciously or unconsciously, especially if they don't have happy marriages themselves. There is a common saying "Misery loves company".

Gladys' daughter Thelisia said once when she was a teenager, "Show me your friends, and I'll show you your future". It was a very profound statement to come from a teenager, but it is so true. Gladys advises us to surround ourselves with positive people who want something out of life. People who don't think that the world owes them everything and are willing to get up every morning taking action to bring more happiness to their lives. She advises staying away from people who are easily influenced by others' opinions. They will be our friends today and our enemies tomorrow, just because they heard something about us.

Gladys used to tell her kids "Not everyone is your friend, baby! You will meet a lot of acquaintances, but you will very seldom have a friend". They used to look at her shocked! Gladys is now 75 and she has had only three friends in her life. Her criteria for a friendship are high. She believes that a friend is a person who will lay down their life for you, and we are not going to find that every day. She sees a friend as someone who, if they see a truck coming and it's going to hit you, they will push you out of the way, even if it means they might get hit by it, because they love you and they're your friend. And so, not everybody is your friend.

Gladys believes that people may get close to us to see what we can give them, or to get some information they can use later for their own benefit, regardless of whether doing so will cause harm to us. Gladys thinks it is safer not to share your feelings and thoughts with everyone, because some people may turn on you, to hurt you by using those thoughts and feelings against you.

That's exactly why I am writing this book. To diffuse hatred and the war that is happening between people, who are trying to push each other, or hurt each other due to internal insecurities. The only way to do this is by infusing love. By loving the self so deeply that we feel secure no matter what comes up in life. And having the same love for others.

Gladys adds that we meet a lot of nice people in our lives. Not all of them are meant to stay with us for the long term. Some people come to our lives for a reason and others for a season, but very few are there to stay forever. When we accept that fact, it will give us a lot of relief. There is a tree analogy of people written by Tyler Perry that says:

Some people like leaves on a tree.
They are there for a season
And then they're gone.
And while they're there, they're really there
And when they leave, they're gone.

And then there's some that like the root of the tree.
They will always be there.
As the root is not going anywhere.

Gladys' message to all ladies is "You weren't born Siamese twins, so you don't need a man to complete you. You only need to learn how to love yourself before you can love someone else. You need to know who you are before you can present yourself to somebody else. And in doing that it means you have to learn to live with you, the real you, not who the world thinks you are, and not who your parents tried to make you into being, but who you are! Only then you can make someone else happy, but that person has to know the real you". Gladys' biological daughter Thelisia is just as strong and independent as her mother. She left a man she wasn't happy with and is raising her kids alone. Her mom is so proud of her.

Gladys adds that it is so important to be honest, because the other person is either going to like you or not going to like you. If they don't like you, keep them moving and look for the next. This doesn't mean anyone is better than the other, it just means that they are not for each other. Be totally honest with yourself and whomever you meet and don't hold back anything about yourself. Feel secure, because if you are not doing so, it is as if you don't love who you are. It's either all of you that you love or none of you.

Remember, in order to have a good relationship, you need to be honest. If you tell the truth about what you want, what you expect, what you want to receive, and what you don't want to receive, then you never have to compromise. And if you are being totally honest and it doesn't work out, then it means you haven't met the right person yet. It does not mean you should stop being honest. You never need to question whether to say something or not, just be kind while saying it. You don't have to be blunt or hurt someone else's feelings, but if you feel like saying something, just say it.

When I asked Gladys about a metaphor for her fairy-tale with this amazing man James, she said, "It is the truth about love". As I see it, "Yes, it is!" It signifies the truth about loving herself, all of herself, unconditionally, and then connecting to her soulmate with love, raising their kids with love, treating the older generation embodied in her mom with love, and bridging to the whole world with all of those fostering kids with love.

Grandma celebrating her 99th birthday

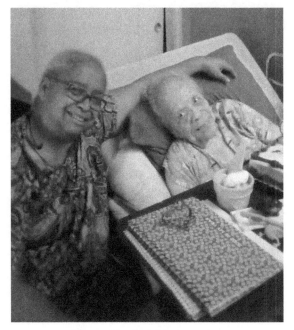

Mama Glayds with Grandma

CHAPTER 2

Surviving Loss

Grief is the emotional contract of both death and divorce. Surviving them and becoming ready to live a happy life, where you can experience love again, will require you to go through the natural steps of the process, by travelling through the dark tunnel to the other end of it.

"The risk of love is loss, and the price of loss is grief...
But the pain of grief is only a shadow when compared
with the pain of never risking love."

— HILARY STANTON ZUNIN

When people lose their adored soulmate due to death or divorce, they often make unconscious promises that they will never allow love to find its way to their hearts again. They become afraid of another loss one day, followed by pain and hurt. To protect themselves, they close their hearts so tightly, not allowing any sweet emotion to get in or come out. But by doing this they are truncating a crucial part of their soul and hindering the fullness of their life experience. If they choose to open their hearts, however, the power of love has an extraordinary capacity to fuel them with the energy required to do the unexpected, while at the same time bringing the joy and ecstasy their wounded souls crave for in life.

By the end of this chapter, you will be able to build a new perspective about loss and find different ways to deal with it. You will know that it is the inevitable truth that no human being on earth can escape, as it happens to all of us at some point in our lives. You will also understand what happens when people are hit by this sad truth, and how they remain stuck in their unexpressed emotions. You'll learn how to break free from them, to start regaining some power to pursue life again.

You will also understand that love does not hurt, and divorce or separation does not have to be painful, either for the couple or their children. A healthy divorce is much better than sustaining a dysfunctional marriage that has reached a dead end. I will also share with you the stories of people who have survived such losses in life. When they decided to learn the lessons of what happened and move forward, their lives flourished beyond limits.

It is important to understand that no matter what we do, how angry we are about loss, how sad or guilty we feel, the dead cannot return, and we must live our lives as it was written for us, the number of days and years we are meant to live after this loss. Even if we choose to act like dead people, closing our hearts, turning ourselves into machines without feelings, we will still be living those days and years. We will be responsible for how we live them and what we do in them. We will be asked about it all.

Several months ago, I lost a dear uncle who people would call an angel, after he suffered from brain cancer for many years. Although he went into a coma before his death, I was still hoping that he would be one of those rare cases that come back, recover from illness and start living a normal life with his kids. But it did not happen.

People might think that we have been prepared already for this loss. Guess what? We are never prepared to lose a beloved! Our minds just can't cope with it easily. The grief process must take place no matter what. So, I cried and cried, kept thinking about how he had been unable to enjoy his life with his kids for several years, how patient, kind and wise he was…

At one point I started thinking about the lessons of this loss and what I might do about them. Only then I was able to start regaining some power in my life. I understand that when the lost one is a sibling, a parent, a son or daughter, or a spouse the pain is much more severe. But being a sensitive and empathic person who feels other people's emotions, this was tough on me too. And it was not the first loss I had experienced in my lifetime.

Grieving the death of a beloved

We keep being hit by the unexpected in life, putting us in a foggy mental state and creating a lot of confusion. Death, among all, is the most profound experience. It is too scary; we don't want to think about it at all, yet it is inescapable. Our minds try many times in despair to figure out why or how this could happen to us. And what to do about it. This happens unwillingly. We struggle to deal with it and don't know how to overcome it. Lots and lots of questions requiring logical answers collide with each other in our minds, overwhelming us with thoughts and feelings and causing us to become physically exhausted.

As with my uncle, even when our beloved suffers from a terminal illness, when death happens it still has a shocking effect on our minds and souls. We start wondering, "Is this it?! Is this the end of it?! Can we reverse it?!". And the sad answer is "Unfortunately, no". Death is an irreversible loss that, as much as we hate, we must deal with gracefully. We must continue our lives with peace, hoping that we can one day meet our lost beloved in heaven. To do this, grief must undergo its natural stages and take its time.

Stages of grief

Stage 1: Avoid denial ("No, this cannot be true!") and accept the fact that death has happened. Denial is the mind's easiest coping mechanism with any harsh reality.

Stage 2: Avoid utilizing distractions to run away from your emotions. This will not do you any good; instead, it works against you. It is like closing a pressurized cooking pan while it is full of steam. These emotions may manifest as illness or explode in a way that may damage many aspects of your life.

Stage 3: Mourn, and allow the hard emotions like anger, fear, sadness and confusion to come to the surface. Be present with all of those emotions and treat them as respectful guests.

Stage 4: Understand that the pain of loss may keep revisiting you from time to time. Be aware of it when it happens, and deal with it with the delicacy it requires.

While grieving, people may keep oscillating between a desire to move forward and their loyalty to the lost beloved who they feel deserves more mourning. This is okay. They may even be pulled back by the fear of experiencing loss again, causing them to avoid developing loving attachments towards anyone else. Even when they decide to finally move forward, spikes of grief may find their way to their hearts, as they recall memories about their lost beloved, which can be stimulated by uncontrollable triggers.

The time it takes to mourn and move forward depends on the strength of the emotional attachment and literacy about death. By that I mean how we think about death, our willingness to accept it as a fact of life, and how to deal with it. I met people in their forties and fifties who could not overcome the loss of a dear parent since childhood. They held unconscious believes about it that kept manifesting in their habitual reactions, behaviors and chronic illnesses due to the old trapped emotions.

I heard a story about a teenager whose dear friend's death threw him into a realm. He started having limited interactions with his parents. His father got worried and started looking for help. After listening carefully to what the father's friend had to say, I suspected that there was an emotional void between the teenager and his parents, or probably between the parents themselves, causing him to get strongly attached to that friend who meant the world to him.

When the friend died, the teenager decided to cover himself with a thick shell, as a form of protection, because the loss was too painful for him to tolerate. It is important to watch out for any social withdrawal symptoms you may develop, due to the severity of the experience, in order to protect yourself, or to make sense of all what happened. If so, take your time but don't indulge in the situation too long, as it may lead to depression.

Anger is one of the most profound emotions people can carry in their hearts, yet they can hardly express it in the case of death. It could be accumulated anger from life events together that was never expressed. It may also be feeling angry that their beloved left them alone in life. The problem in such cases is that anger is usually accompanied with guilt and shame about the reaction. "How come I am feeling this way?! It is the truth of life, and GOD's decision to take their soul at this exact moment and time. How can I feel angry about it?!".

Then comes the fear of expressing anger or talking about it – because the surrounding society may not be understanding or supportive. It may even blame them for expressing such emotions, letting them feel ashamed and abandoned. They end up feeling lonelier than they were. How harsh can this be to the soul?

According to Gay and Kathlyn Hendricks, the best way to get past a loss is by navigating through it, allowing yourself to shift the focus from your mind to your body, and expressing all types of emotions that you are feeling. Then check your willingness to close the chapter of that loss, to create a new life. When you are ready, move forward. This is exactly what Theresa Du Toit did to create the glorious new life she is living now, after mourning two loving husbands. You will be able to read her story at the end of this chapter.

Remember, as we go through this process great gifts will come with it. The first is our immense ability to accept ourselves with all emotions that arise with loss and develop more compassion towards self and others. The second gift is to appreciate life and sink into a deeper loving state with all people who are in it now.

Moving forward after divorce

Throughout life I have come across many people adapting harmful or unpleasant behaviours, like different kinds of addiction, narcissism, aggression, cynicism ...etc. I have often heard excuses like "She got divorced", "His parents were divorced when he was a kid" or "His wife left him".

I kept wondering, why is divorce so ugly that it corrupts people's behaviours? Why do these behaviours seem to be the most stable and unchangeable ones? Is it because they come under a valid excuse? And what makes it so valid? Does divorce have to be destructive? Is it a must that anyone who undergoes divorce or is raised with a divorced parent develops maladaptive behaviours? If so, then why risk getting married, if the last available solution to an unsuccessful marriage will be so painful and destructive?

I had those questions in my head until I attended a course with a public figure who got divorced. He then got happily married to another lady and is still having a great relationship with his ex-wife. How is this possible? Well, when he and his ex-wife realized that their marriage was reaching a dead end, he got terrified and started thinking about all the bad things that divorce would bring to the family: losing time with his kids, their gatherings and prayers together; the possibility of being blamed by his kids for the separation; and the possibility of them hating him if their mother said bad things about him.

He kept thinking, how could he go through the process in the most pleasurable way for him, his ex-wife and their kids altogether? He figured out that the solution was to become friends with his ex-wife. I know hearing this may initially seem strange. You may ask "If it was possible for them to become friends, why they got divorced in the first place?". I guess there is a fine line that separates a happy friendship from a happy intimate relationship.

He made sustaining a great friendship with his ex-wife his top priority. He stayed patient whenever she said something and bit his tongue many times to stop himself from saying anything bad about her to the kids – so that she would not say something bad about him in return. As tough as the process was, it was incredibly fruitful.

And now he is happily married again, his ex-wife is in a happy relationship, and all of them gather at the same home to take care of the kids whenever they are ill and need some care. When there is a wish, there is a way. Thanks to him for breaking us free from an unhelpful belief and leading us by example.

What if you have already survived a tough divorce? The solution is still there, and it comes by first understanding this analogy: when a person has cancerous cells developing around an organ and the surgeon recommends removing them, then surgery becomes the painful must-have course of treatment.

Yes, you will deal with post-surgery pain. After all, it was part your body, and it is lost now. Imagine if you continued living with this malfunctioning organ, and cancer spread all over your body, what would be the consequence? So, consider that what happened has happened. You survived it, and now you have the chance to be reborn into a new human.

Give yourself the permission to draw a smile on your face even during the darkest times. As tough as it seems, and even if it is not an authentic smile, it will still trick your mind and automatically shift it into a better state. Do this as much as you can, to accumulate more happy moments into your life. Allow yourself to live and experience each moment as it passes with all your senses, believing that GOD will bring you happier moments, and that you will be able to get out of this darkness, if you are willing and ready to do it. In the coming pages, you will see how Khaled Abul-Dahab turned his divorce and the losses that came with it into a triumph and created a happy life.

Exercise 2.1: Muscle progression relaxation

People with trapped emotions tend to have tensed muscles, hindering their ability to create and visualize easily. This exercise will work as a preparation to exercise 4.2, to relax your muscles and ease the visualization.

1. Lie down in a comfortable place and close your eyes.
2. Take a few deep breaths and send a message to your brain that you want your body to relax.
3. Focus on each muscle of your body, one at a time.
4. Start with your forehead, eyes and cheeks. Tense them as tightly as you can, and then release.
5. Move to your neck and jaw. Tense them as tightly as you can and then release.
6. Follow the same process with your whole body, until you reach your feet and toes.
7. Make sure to keep breathing.
8. Once done, you will experience a bit of relaxation in your muscles and will be ready to go to the next exercise.

Exercise 2.2: Receiving the loving messages

In this exercise you will locate your trapped emotions and listen to the messages they are carrying with love. Before doing so, I encourage you to watch the videos in the additional resources about emotions and the human brain, which will help you a lot during the visualization.

1. Once you complete exercise 4.1, stay in the same position where you are feeling relaxed. But ensure to keep your mind alert and don't fall asleep.
2. Turn your focus inward to your organs and call your angry emotion.
3. Check where is it located in your body. Ask it what message it is carrying to you with love. And how you can satisfy it.
4. Listen carefully with respect and without arguments.
5. Thank it for the message and promise to do your best to satisfy its need.
6. Now, call your sad emotion and repeat steps 3–5. If it requires you to cry, allow yourself to do so until you feel relieved.
7. Ask if any other emotions want to voice themselves and ask them about their loving messages.
8. Promise them to take immediate actions, and to do what is best for all of you (your physical body, emotions, soul and heart).
9. If there was pain before doing the exercise, see how it has changed after doing it.
10. If the pain was eased or disappeared with the exercise, then the message was delivered successfully.
11. If the pain is still there, then maybe you want to revisit it for more information.

12. I want you to understand that sometimes those emotions will start arguing, judging and rejecting each other. That is okay; let them do so and only watch without interfering or favouring one over the other, as all of them are valuable parts of you.
13. Repeat these exercises as many times as you can, and whenever you feel stuck or in pain.

Caution: if pain persists after doing the exercises 2-3 times, you may want to consult a doctor to ensure there is no physical or biological illness. And if you are currently suffering from depression or intense emotions, ensure to consult a professional practitioner before doing any of the exercises. Because in such cases you will require a lot of external support while overcoming your grief, before being able to do anything alone.

Additional resources

- ♥ Get to know your emotions video:
  https://youtu.be/nTII0cyUbQo
- ♥ The human brain (episodes 1–3)
  https://youtu.be/Xmah1wUiGuU
  https://youtu.be/M4CFFrGrylc
  https://youtu.be/56N2R0VsTWI

The more you hold onto your emotions and suppress them during grief or while overcoming divorce, the worse your experience in life can be and the harder it becomes to move forward. Blockages get so deep in your body that you forget they even exist. Those emotions get confined in the weakest organs in the body and produce symptoms of illness that in many cases have no other physical or biological cause.

To survive such losses, you need to be willing to express all kinds of emotions without shame or guilt. Find a friend, a family member or a professional who can provide you with the space required to express and share all your thoughts without criticism, someone who is willing to remain present while those emotions are surfacing. Treat your emotions with respect even if they are painful, then give yourself the permission to experience something new or different in life.

It may help you to know that whatever you choose is understandable, whether it is to grieve longer or to allow the experience to remain where it is, in peace, while moving forward. Everyone has their own pace and their own timing. Also, remember that we have limited time on earth, and whether we choose to bury ourselves with the lost beloved or choose to move on, we will be held responsible for our life and asked about it.

I know it is scary to just think about the idea, let alone talking about it, and no comforting words may seem enough, but as sensitive as the topic is, we must tackle it and give it the respect and time it deserves. Death is the inevitable fact of life that no one can escape. It is a shocking visitor that comes with a variety of emotions. If these emotions are not expressed and dealt with in compassion, they can create blockages that hinder people from connecting to themselves or others and make them unable to move forward.

It is also important to understand that a healthy divorce is better than a dysfunctional marriage. Because in the absence of love, people have an extraordinary capacity to do evil work. Love cannot be a constant drain to your energy and heart, it rather revives them. It is possible to make divorce an easy experience if we wish to. This will save the couple from carrying any toxic residues from the relationship or passing it to their children.

Make sure to do all the exercises in this chapter and the previous one many times. And whenever you experience a spike of sadness after moving forward, come back and do them again. We are all human; emotions are parts of us that we cannot discard. You are not alone in this journey. All of us are wounded in one way or another. When someone or something wants to end their time in your life, allow it to happen without resistance. Surrender to the new that is coming your way, trusting that things and people who eliminate themselves from your life were just preparing you for something bigger. If their return is meant to happen, it will happen in a better shape and context, after you have grown into a much happier and wiser human.

After releasing that painful baggage with respect, it is time to learn about different forms of love. They include reclaiming the lost treasure of your passions from childhood, discovering new passions, and activating all of them in your new life. In the coming chapters you will learn all of this and more. You will learn about love misconceptions; this is when people trick themselves, mistakenly thinking that they love themselves when what they are really doing is adding layers over the ashes, due to the fears of dealing with their issues. Feeling excited? Let's move on.

The Transformational Love

*"Love never dies, it gets transformed into
different forms and shapes."*

— REEM AHMED

*I*n this bubbly story you will learn how human love can
be transformed into a deep connection with a career
passion – with the potential of being transformed again into
a uniquely intimate relationship with another human. I met
Theresa Du Toit (the destination wedding celebrant) at an event
I participated in while studying my wedding planning course
at the beginning of 2017.

While I was standing with my lovely colleagues in the
academy, Theresa arrived with her vibrant energy and was
introduced to us by one of the academy managers. On the spot
Theresa looked at me in the eyes and said "Reem you have a
wonderful soul and energy, keep it!". At that moment I felt
astonished, I opened my eyes with surprise and thought "Oh my
GOD! She saw me! Even though she does not know me!". I took
an immediate decision to get to know this beautiful lady better.

I stayed in touch with Theresa on social media and through
casual communications on WhatsApp from time to time.
When the time came to write my book about loving and happy
relationships, I could not spare her story. Her happiness was so
evident and illuminating to everything around her. I wanted

to learn the secret of this happiness and inspire people with it by passing her secret on to them.

Theresa's story started with her husband Nick. They met after Theresa had mourned her deceased and fantastic first husband. Nick was coming out of two divorces, causing him to shut off his heart. Theresa was still full of life and open to getting married again; it was astonishing to Nick. His tough relationship experience had brought him pain that he did not want to go through again, but for Theresa it just meant that GOD still wanted something more for her. Surprisingly enough within six weeks of meeting Theresa, Nick decided to open his heart again as he fell in love with her. By the end of those six weeks, he was proposing to her.

Theresa lived an amazing marriage with Nick. It was so full of love, understanding and happiness that his kids from previous marriages used to ask her what she had done to their father to change him so much! I think the answer is clear, it was his willingness to open his heart and connect with the absolutely fabulous Theresa. Her energy is so inviting, and she has the capacity to embrace almost every human between her wings.

Two years and four months later, Nick was driving in the desert and suddenly had a heart attack. He stepped off his quad bike and immediately dropped dead. It was shocking news for Theresa. She became extremely sad and took time to mourn the loss of her beloved Nick. One year after this sad event she experienced a shift inside her. She started thinking that there is something more to do in life than sinking in our sad feelings. She was waiting for the call but did not know what it would be, or how she would receive it.

She was dreaming about something beautiful to come forth out of a bad thing that happened, which was her loving husband's death. She suspected it would be something related to public speaking, as she wanted to share her story to give hope to others. Theresa was sure enough that she did not want to have a job where she would be reporting to a boss anymore. She tried it and never enjoyed it, so it was time for her to become the boss of herself.

One day her daughter's friend, a wedding photographer, told Theresa "I know that you love people and are so passionate about public speaking. Why don't you become a wedding celebrant? You could be perfect at it". At that time Theresa did not know what a wedding celebrant meant, but she was ready for the call! She started googling wedding celebrations, to learn more about them and explore what a celebrant does.

The more she learned about it, the more she fell in love with it, and the more she believed it was meant for her. She became so passionate about marriages and their celebrations that she decided to become one of those celebrants who do not only celebrate the happiness of a couple, but also make their celebration unique by speaking their own story.

Theresa communicated her wish to become a wedding celebrant to her friend in Dubai who was a website developer. She got so excited for Theresa that she decided to build her website as a gift without any charges, but she asked Theresa to write her own content, and it was easy for Theresa to do so. Theresa was in love with what she was doing, as marriages are full of love and passion, and reflect Theresa's vibrant energy. Initially, she did not have photos of events to include in her website, as she was just starting out, so as a tribute to her deceased husband Nick and to her love story with this amazing man, she added their pictures on the website. Once the website went live, everything fell into place from there.

Theresa started her official practice as a wedding celebrant in December 2016 with a Muslim couple, for whom she prepared a Western ceremony with an Arabic style. She brought a lot of love, life and wisdom to the wedding because she knew what it means to have a happy and amazing marriage. She believed that what she does during those ceremonies is an opportunity to help couples build beautiful marriages that sustain over time, where love only grows and is never reduced.

One day Theresa got a call from someone in Bahrain to do a distance wedding ceremony. When she got the call, she started thinking "This is a fantastic opportunity! I want to do more of these". As she is fond of travelling, she started fantasizing about becoming an international distance-wedding celebrant, one who travels all over the globe to celebrate love and happy marriages. Her second distant wedding was for a couple in Sri Lanka. Then she did another one in South Africa and planned to do one in Georgia by the end of 2020.

Theresa loves celebrating weddings outdoors. It is the preference for Western weddings, and at the same time it reflects her connection to nature and fondness for the sea. Despite knowing that such things can only be done during winter in Dubai, she did not experience any fears of having drops or fluctuations in her business during other seasons. She took a wise decision to follow the weather anywhere in the world, and whenever possible she will travel to celebrate the weddings of her couples in nature. When Theresa decided that nothing would stop her from doing what she wants, she started falling in love with the unknown. In the unknown lies greatness and new possibilities.

Theresa feels absolute joy, excitement, and positive energy whenever she celebrates a wedding. Knowing without doubt that this is right for her, she is so passionate about it. Another inspiring secret about this amazing soul, who I can only look at with admiration for the natural smile in her eyes, is that she is now ready to welcome a new soulmate. She is calling him from the unknown and sending him her love and kisses every day, without knowing who he is or how he will come to her. She trusts that he is there somewhere. With absolute certainty she'll meet him one day, and every passing day is bringing them closer to each other.

Theresa celebrating a wedding in the desert!

The Beautiful Rebirth

"Out of every crisis, there is a chance to be reborn."

— Dr Barbra De Angelis

The star of this story is someone I truly respect. He is someone who taught me a new meaning for the word professionalism, and how getting into the mood is all we need to produce creative arts. When I moved to consultancy services and started my job as a water engineer, I felt the world had opened new possibilities to me. I wanted to cultivate my creative skills. I believe that we can bring art and science together into one place, and we don't have to operate from only one hemisphere of our brains if we appreciate both.

When I was looking for a professional photography coach, I was guided to Khaled Abul-Dahab. I found out that he comes from an engineering background! He is so passionate about photography. And he has determined to deliver to the world a precious message about creation, which you will discover through this story. I felt impressed and thought that he must be an excellent photographer! Khaled had the habit of interviewing students before signing them up to the course, to define expectations and let us know more about what we will learn, and how we will learn it. That was intriguing to me!

When I discovered that we'd be taking our classes in the field (i.e., beaches, vegetable markets, etc.) I felt a lot of hesitation.

I was very shy and closed to myself. Being in an open area in places that might be new to me, with people I didn't know was a scary idea to me. Khaled sensed it. He was so understanding and respectful of my culture and background. He started telling me that all the students in my group would be women, and that all of them were from decent families he knew himself. I registered for the course. It was one of the best decisions I took in my life, and the outcome exceeded my expectations.

When Khaled asked us in the first class how we define professional photography, we gave many answers, but none of them was what he was looking for. So, he told us his definition "It is when we are able to take a photo with the camera that is exactly like what our eyes are seeing, same colours, same lines, and at the same time it is appealing to the viewer! Without much editing after the photo is taken". I was amused! Any excellent photographer will know the amount of work required to achieve this outcome, and how tough it can be sometimes with the unexpected changes of light and weather.

Khaled taught us how to stand, how to hold the camera, and how to move to get the shot in a particular way, or to capture the movement of an object. It was an amazing journey. All of us were proud at the end of what we did and achieved. When I wanted to dedicate a section in my book about how falling in love with something and being passionate about it can help us overcome tough times in life, I immediately thought of this creative soul, who is so passionate about photography. He teaches all its secrets, and his comprehensive knowledge about it comes from the heart. He wants people to treat it with care and respect and produce photos as beautiful as his. And he always becomes proud of his students!

Khaled's love story to photography started in childhood. He bought his first camera at a very young age and used to take photos of events for his family. He also worked as a model to be shot by other photographers. Photography was a hobby that he wanted to cultivate. He never thought it would become his profession one day. In fact, Khaled had multiple creative skills. He started his journey with music, then acting, then poetry and writing, and then caricature drawings as expressions of emotions and mood. These were put in an exhibition in the area where he lived. Finally came photography, which grew inside him throughout the years without him even realizing it.

Khaled was blessed with a great mother who always believed in him, supported him, and attended all the plays he acted in just to see him happy. In 2003 a turning point came in the way that Khaled viewed photography when he was working at a marketing company and invited some international photographers. During a meeting with them, Khaled was astonished by their work and felt that his knowledge in photography was modest compared to what he saw, despite what people were saying about his talent. That was the first spark of photography as a possible profession. He saw its true potential and decided to dive deeper into this amazing field to learn about it more.

Khaled got a job at a bank in Dubai and moved there in 2005. By that time, photography started becoming a dear friend who speaks to him and understands him, a companion to express all what goes on inside him. Every Friday morning Khaled would get up at 7 am and go to the sea to start his date with his lover (the camera and its shots). He would get into the mood and enjoy living in it. He mentioned that he enjoyed the camera's company more than his ex-wife, as it understood him and spoke to him more. When he used to have migraine, he would take his camera and unite with the beauty of nature through photography, and his headache would disappear.

Khaled's mission of delivering his message about photography to people started in 2009, and it was a long way to travel. He lost his job in the bank due to the Great Recession. It is true that he had never enjoyed this job, as he was doing it for others and not for himself, but it was his only source of income at that time. The bank fired him after three and a half years of hard and dedicated work, blocked his accounts, and asked him to pay his loans. This happened just ten days before he divorced his wife.

Khaled was thrown into the street, feeling lost and betrayed, not knowing what to do. Then he remembered his mom who had always believed in him and defended him to his father. He immediately decided to start the journey of forming a company with the remaining AED 650 in his pocket, both to do what he had always loved to do and to prove to his mom that he deserved all her support. He invested the money in producing flyers and put them on cars in the city, to tell people about his photography work.

Starting a company from scratch with no financial support, while being under the stress of having a loan to pay before leaving the country (or ending up in jail) was one of the biggest challenges in Khaled's life. His high morals told him to stay and clear his debt in the right way. Even if he did not succeed in clearing his loan and had to go to jail, he would go happily, knowing that he was working at something he loved.

Not long after Khaled lost his job, his friend was preparing an advertisement about casting for the company where he was working. They had a problem with the lighting, so Khaled offered to do the lighting work for them. They did not have photography in the advertisement at that time, so Khaled did that for them too. The project was very successful, and Khaled used it to start marketing himself more. When people started buying his work and paying well for it, it created the second spark for him. It proved the value of what he was doing. His confidence doubled and he was motivated to continue the journey.

Khaled dreamt of becoming successful in his career in photography and becoming a global photographer. He worked so hard to make this dream come true. He travelled to many countries for work, but he could not travel back home to Egypt to see his mom, who was still supporting him from a distance, believing in him as she always did, and keeping him in her prayers without waiting for anything in return and without any guarantees. Her only motivation was unconditional love for her son and a desire for him to be happy.

Because he could not see his mom for two and a half years, he decided to go live on TV all the time so that she could see him. It was both exhausting and scary, as it required from him a lot of achievements to talk about. He had to do TV interviews every week and made 120 interviews all over the world. In one year, Khaled became the highest-paid and most famous photographer in Dubai.

From being a fired employee who lost his salary of AED 3000 per month and being unable to travel to see his mom or talk to her, he started gaining much more income than his lost salary. He gained a reputation and appreciation at a worldwide scale and started having international calls with his mom every single day, even before the age of free online calling. And despite being away, he was still tender and kind to his family. After two years and seven months of his journey with photography, and all the tough events he had to overcome, his sister brought to his attention that he hadn't travelled back to Egypt to see his family for almost three years. He immediately booked a ticket after speaking with her and went to see his family within one week of that call.

Khaled started having international students flying to Dubai just to take his photography courses. He felt so grateful for all of those blessings that he never imagined would happen and were beyond his dreams' ceiling. He just wanted to be successful in photography and to pay his debt. He had not expected all these gifts from Allah. He recalls a time when he dreamt about participating in Taira's show for America's Got Talent. At that time his assistant did not believe that he could become a global photographer, but he did.

The first international call he got after posting his videos on YouTube was from a company in the US that was marketing for teaching systems. They loved his work and invited him to teach his photography courses at Columbia University, through them, for six months. Although the project was not completed, it inspired him and affirmed his value internationally. He was motivated to participate in a competition in the US and got his second worldwide shot award. Motivation was the top drive for all his achievements. After winning that competition in the US he went to Italy, had an interview on MBC TV, and had a lot of work in many other countries.

When Khaled wanted to work on projects in other countries, he had lots of fear and hesitated to leave his business in Dubai, because he would be investing a lot of money from his own pocket. He weighed the results to see whether it would be good enough for him, then he took the leap. He also experienced fear when he used to create his courses, as he wasn't sure if people would like them, but he knew deep inside that he wanted to do it. He used to take videos for himself while he was creating those courses. It was an interesting journey with a mixture of feelings and an amazing taste.

What kept Khaled moving forward despite all his fears was his strong belief that we are here on earth to support and inspire each other. We humans are weak and need each other. For him, photography was the way to help people see the beauty of Allah's creation and understand how it can change their lives. It supports us and elevates our souls. Photography helped Khaled enjoy things more. He could see through photography what people cannot see, especially that we can't control anything in nature. He always felt the need to do more work on a shot to produce an artistic outcome, one to make people say, "I have seen this several times before, but it's the first time I see it this way".

Photography brought him closer to GOD. He used to pray and cry during his photography sessions whenever he sensed the amazing creativity of the drawings crafted by Allah on earth. He looks at the beauty of nature as something that washes us from inside. If he could deliver this message to people through photography, then it would be amazing work. He feels he is on Earth for this mission. If he went back and had the choice to live another life, he would still choose this one, which prepared him for all the success and beauty he is experiencing now.

The international award wining photographer Khalid

CHAPTER 3

Roadmap to Self-Love

*Embrace true love, defeat misconceptions,
and reclaim what makes your soul sing.*

*"To be yourself in a world that is so consistently
trying to make you something else,
is the greatest accomplishment."*

— RALPH WALDO EMERSON

"What is self-love, Reem?" you may ask. "How do I know if I love myself or I don't? How do I know if someone else is loving themselves or not?". My answer is "Ask your heart, is it in pain and agony? Or dancing with joy? How about your bodily sensations? Are you relaxed and serene? Or feeling agitated all the time? How about your mind? Is it calm and rested? Or is it jumping restlessly from one thought to another, not allowing you to even sleep well at night?".

This chapter is your blueprint to self-love. You will be introduced to different forms of self-love and be able to know when you are exercising it and when you are not. You will also know when people are fooling themselves, saying that they love themselves when in fact they are covering their deepest pain and agony with a façade – and believing that by doing so, they are released from the responsibility of doing what it takes to genuinely love themselves. Yes, self-love it is a responsibility! In fact, it is a huge one. Going through this chapter, you will come to know what this means.

You will revisit the little child you were, exploring the parts that were lost along the way and the ones that silently developed inside without you being aware of them. You will go on a journey of discovery towards the self. You will dig deeper and elevate higher in your consciousness. The more you learn about yourself and love it, the happier, calmer, safer, more relaxed and serene you will become. I invite you to put what you are learning from this book in practice, even when it seems confusing or strange. When people I know did it, their lives were changed magnificently.

People used to tell me "Love yourself, Reem" and I used to feel confused. I kept thinking "But I do love myself! What do they mean?!". Everyone was making this statement in a commanding way, as if it were only the push of a button. But they only said *what* to do without explaining *how* to do it. Most of the time they would not even tell me what I was doing that gave them the impression that I needed to love myself. What did I need to stop doing, or do differently, to become a person who is deeply and truly in love with herself? A person who people will feel compelled to approach, talk to, give to, and connect with at all levels.

I remember registering for a course, and I was feeling excited and happy about it. I started giving and giving endlessly, consciously and unconsciously. Giving my support, time, affirmations, energy, encouragement, helping others with knowledge, tools and techniques…etc. People were happy and told me nice words like "You are a beautiful person, you have a nice soul, you are very supportive…etc". It made me feel good, but that feeling wouldn't last. So, I would give again to hear those comforting words. I was stuck in this cycle until one day I realized that what I felt was instant gratification, and not true happiness or even genuine love.

I was always waiting for something to happen to feel energized and happy about myself, and when it didn't, I would feel sad, disappointed and drained. All my energy went out and I did not get anything in return to refill my tank! That was purely conditional love. If people responded positively, it meant it was okay for me to love myself and experience those good feelings. But if they didn't, then I would not give myself the permission to feel happy. I was giving the control of my happiness to others.

What if someone I was giving a lot to had issues? What if they did not like me, or were feeling jealous? Was I giving them my keys to use them against me? Was this something I wanted for my life? Of course not. I started searching for what was happening in my inner world. Why did I feel happy when I felt happy? And why did I feel sad when I felt sad? What did I truly want? How do I want to feel? I started exercising what I am bringing to you in this chapter, which put me in a much more peaceful state. And better people started appearing in my life.

I asked in a social media group "What does self-love mean to you? How can you decide whether you love yourself or whether someone else loves himself/herself?" I got a variety of answers, including having "me time", prioritizing myself, cultivating inner peace and feeling centred, taking care of my body and health through drinking plenty of water, getting proper nutrition, sleeping well, exercising, self-consciousness and knowing who I am at the core, learning to say no when I need to, doing things that make me happy and not being pressured to do something out of fear of being disliked.

And this intriguing answer came from one of the members: "Funny, I was at a conference and they asked us to name ten people we love. Rarely did anyone include themselves, I didn't either, but now I am aware. It is an issue for sure for most". Indeed, this is a universal issue, but it can definitely be cured with awareness and diligent actions. During my exploration journey of love, peace, happiness and true fulfilment, I have dived inward to find the lovely loving me, to bring more of it to the surface in my daily life. And that is my wish for you.

Forms of self-love

Self-Love is a very broad term. It can take different shapes and forms. Gratitude, for example, is a form of self-love. Research shows that being grateful elicits the most powerful emotion on earth, which enhances our health and total wellbeing (happiness). Forgiveness is another form of self-love, whether it is towards the self or another person, about a single event or a sequence of events.

Regardless of the cause, releasing this painful memory is necessary to reclaim our inner peace. As we practise forgiveness we need to forget too; they work hand in hand. Forgiveness releases the trapped energy that might be clogging our love channel but doing it without forgetting will allow the stored memory to regenerate itself, causing us to suffer. Choosing to forgive and forget allows us to release the baggage of hurt and grudge from our shoulders. It is a heavy burden that will restrict us from moving forward, hindering our progress.

Let us say, you played a sport, broke your leg and had a strong pain. If you kept remembering what happened, blamed yourself or others, and relived the pain even after your physical recovery, without being able to conquer your fears, how likely are you going to play this game again? In many cases the probability will be low. What if this sport was the passion of your life, and succeeding in it will bring you joy, pride, satisfaction, money...etc., but your painful memory and the fear of experiencing pain again is preventing you from playing it? What are the consequences you are paying, for not forgiving yourself or whoever caused the accident to happen, and not forgetting the old experience? It's a life worth pay.

It is important to understand that forgiveness does not mean condoning the behaviour, having to become friends with the person who hurt you (unless you want to), or inviting them to hurt you again. It rather means being willing and ready to release your attachment to the hurtful memory, to stop it from manifesting in your life again. Holding onto it will cause you to act in a way that invites similar people and situations into your life. And you will continuously relive the same old story until you decide to release it. To exercise self-love, take the wisdom from what happened, learn the lesson that is meant to be learned, and use it for your growth, to become a stronger and happier human. Then choose to release the painful memory with peace.

Feeding our minds with nice thoughts even when things are tough is another form of self-love. It generates feelings that energize us to do what we want in life. Those can be thoughts about ourselves, other people, things, and situations. Doing so allows us to send love towards the whole universe, and lets it give back to us, as what we send out, we shall receive. Another form of self-love is the words we say to ourselves or tell others about us. This gets reinforced with the clothes we wear, the movies we watch, the books we read, and the songs we listen to. All will influence our internal environment and dictate the state of our lives.

Giving different titles to our behaviours like choosing the word "determined" rather than "stubborn" is also a form of self-love. Titles we put on our behaviours affect how we feel, and consequently, our energy levels. We can always choose to release inherited words that do not make us feel good about ourselves. We can be creative and invent something that our mind likes and gives a soothing or energizing effect to our bodies.

Focusing on our circle of control and surrendering after doing our best is another form of self-love. During moments of frustration, trying to control something getting out of hand, we become on edge. We may do things that we may not be so proud of later. By releasing all thoughts and emotions related to controlling the end results we live in a more peaceful world. At the end of the day, whatever is going to happen will happen as life takes its course.

Comparison and competition are some of the worst enemies of self-love. We need to drop them from our lives in all forms and shapes, as we were born to collaborate and build, not to compete and dispute. No one can take a single reward or opportunity that is meant for another person, no matter how hard they try. So, put in the effort that makes you feel satisfied and forget about the results; they are out of your control.

Choosing the right people to spend our time with and staying away from people who deplete our energy is another form of self-love. If someone is constantly putting us down by their words or cold reaction, why spend more time with them?! We can be loving enough to bring what is happening to their attention, as they may not be aware of it. After that, if they insist on repeating the same behaviours with us, then stopping them or eliminating their existence in our lives is a choice we can follow.

Self-love is also found in the discipline to do the things that will serve us and bring long-term happiness, rather than distracting ourselves with what only brings instant gratification (like sleeping more to kill boredom, spending long hours on TV, taking revenge on someone, overeating to compensate for our emotional hunger rather than expressing our needs). I know sometimes you have pain and want to numb it! But running away or numbing pain does not solve the problem. It ruins your future.

Love yourself enough to build your long-term fulfilling goals and look forward in life. If you are waiting for someone to come and motivate you every day to do it, guess what? You'll spend your life waiting. You do not have to jump from one task to another just to feel that you are accomplishing things. If it leaves you exhausted, then you are not helping your body or loving it enough. You need to create a balance between working on your long-term goals and playing and resting. Ask yourself if overcommitting is serving you. What feelings does it elicit? How comfortable does it make you feel? If it brings the best out of you then great. But if not, then you are not exercising enough love towards yourself.

Trying a new mindset or attitude is also a form of self-love. This might be doing or asking for what you want rather than choosing to be ill. It also comes in the form of telling your life story with pride and respect, as this story is what led to the person you are now. Sometimes taking uncomfortable actions shows love towards the self. It allows us to expand our threshold, improves our skills, and takes us to the next level.

Expressing to your friend that you need to finish a call due to other commitments is also a form of self-love. It may initially appear as unloving to the other person, but how loving is staying on the line and giving your friend only partial attention, as your mind is busy thinking about something else? It always helps to put yourself in the position of the other person, and act in the same way you'd want them to act towards you. Choose kind loving words and excuse yourself with respect.

Do not worry about being judged or called selfish. Making yourself a priority is not selfish, it rather shows your capacity to love yourself and others too. In airplanes people are instructed to put on their own masks first before helping their kids. The same happens in healthy relationships, there is a balance between giving and receiving.

Every creature on earth is part of a life cycle; it takes something and gives another thing in return. Water evaporates and returns to the ground in the form of rain. Animals eat food and their waste fertilizes plants. The whole world is based on the concept of giving and receiving to sustain a balance. If we are only giving without receiving there will come a time when we cannot give any more due to physical, mental and emotional exhaustion. Nor we will be able to receive, because others will not know how to give to us. Our time on earth is limited; every minute in our lives counts. We have the choice to live it in a loving or an unloving way to self and others.

While writing this book, I learned to look at people's behaviour towards me as a reflection of my current psychological state. When someone tries to ignore my success or puts me down, I first look to see if this is a pattern in their behaviour. If so, I either shield myself from this toxic behaviour or limit my time with the person. And if not, then I ask myself "What is my internal state now? Am I seeking their approval? Are they reminding me not to seek for it from the outside world? What kind of thoughts I am having today?". It is important to ask these questions especially when receiving the same behaviour from more than one person at the same period of time.

Once I realize what is happening in my inner world and take charge, people who treat me in a way I don't like would step back with total honour and change their behaviours. I advise you not to get trapped in a spiral of thinking, asking "What is wrong with them/me? Did I do something wrong? Why are they doing this?". I have been there and found nothing. Don't waste your time and energy on it; rather start thinking "What can I do to stop eliciting these behaviours from others? How can I stop it from affecting me?". That is a true expression of self-love.

Some people misinterpret pain for lack of self-love, like undergoing a painful treatment, having unpleasant medication, taking an uncomfortable action to change something in their lives, or exercising and eating healthy food. I want to challenge you here by asking "Is this pain temporary or long-term? Which is more persistent, pain from exercising or pain in the bones due to lack of exercising?". I trust your wise mind to give the answer that serves you.

Awareness about the crucial importance of self-love and self-acceptance is spreading with the speed of light. However, we are still seeing a lot of misery around the world. I believe the root cause of it is a lack of feeling responsible to exercise unconditional love towards self and others. We need to think about ourselves and other people in the same way. I have the right to receive as much as I give them, and they have the right to get as much as I receive from them. Then keep the channel of connection open through our spiritual practices.

Love misconceptions

I often see people engaging in maladaptive behaviors and calling it love. They tease their partners by consistently doing things they know make them angry, and call it love. They stalk their partners on their mobiles out of jealousy, they shout or fight and call it love. They may also allow their partners to treat them badly under the name of love. I call those actions "love misconceptions".

People give love a distorted meaning and allow it to dictate their behaviour. It often happens when they have experienced similar behaviour from their parents, caretakers, friends, schoolmates, teachers, etc. when they were growing. Kids don't understand the difference between a loving act and a dysfunctional one. They take whatever is given to them as love, grow up with this misconception, and start treating others the same way or accepting similar behaviours under the name of love.

As self-love takes different shapes and forms, love misconception is the same. Imagine a person who wants everything to be perfectly done, not allowing themself or others to make mistakes, not giving room for deviation from what they want. I hear people say, "I am a perfectionist". I call them "The restless people", whose attention immediately goes to what is missing in something before being able to appreciate anything about it. Like appreciating an act of kindness, a present, a speech, prepared food, paying bills, a constructed road, raising a kid, ...etc. This appreciation can be to themselves, to their spouse, to a friend, a construction company, or an acquaintance they met in the store who helped them find what they wanted.

How often do you say to yourself "Why did s/he do it this way? There are ways to do it better. They could do so and so"? If these are the usual first thoughts popping into your mind, then you are falling into the trap of perfectionism. You may argue that perfectionism is positive, or that you are just seeking improvements. Seeking improvements is great, but to what? What is it that you appreciate and want to improve?

Maybe the building was nice, and the balconies could have been wider. Or the road was well-paved, but there could have been some grass and flowers on the sideway. Is your wife a great mother, cooking and taking care of the household, and you want her to take care of you more? Is your husband doing well in paying the bills and saving you from tolerating a toxic job, and you want him to spend more time with the kids because they need a father figure in their lives?

This pursuit of perfectionism robs the happy moments from your life. The nice moments that you experience when you start appreciating things first. Stealing those moments jeopardizes self-love. You are taking from the self a happy experience that comes with appreciation and replacing it with an unhappy experience by focusing on what is missing. If that is your habitual thinking, then you are stealing from yourself many happy moments, and setting up your mind for less and less self-love – and less and less love towards others.

Wearing a social mask and forcing yourself to appear in a certain way in front of others is a huge love misconception. People think that showing only the parts they think others will like protects them from being rejected. The truth is they are rejecting themselves by feeling ashamed and hiding the parts they dislike. No matter how many masks you create to suit different people, you will never be able to have enough. People in different situations will see your contradictory actions; they'll start doubting and disbelieving you. And they will end up rejecting you, but this time for not being your true self, for hiding it, and not appreciating it enough.

Finding your passions

When you hear the word passion, what is the first thing that comes to your mind? Passion is defined as a strong, uncontrollable emotion, a feeling of intense enthusiasm or a compelling desire for someone or something. In the context of this chapter, I'll focus on passion felt towards a cause, an idea, or a thing.

There are two types of passions. The ones we had as children, and others that we developed along the way. Some are already known to us, and others are yet to be discovered through pondering and observation. Passion makes us feel energized and elated. In order to live a happy congruent life, it is our responsibility to reclaim our lost passions, define the new ones that developed inside us along the way, and put them all into practise every single day.

Let's think for a moment, what were the things that used to interest you as a child and faded along the way? What did you enjoy doing, hiding in your secret place away from everyone and anyone? You spent hours doing it, losing track of time and space.

What did you love telling your uncles and aunts, your family members and friends, every time you saw them? What are the things that make you feel happy and alive when you do them or talk about them? What were the things that you felt drawn to from inside, before being influenced by societal rules and opinions?

And now as an adult, what are the things that you spend hours of your time surfing the internet or social media for? What occupies your mind day and night, and you keep dreaming about all the time? Day dreaming, and even while sleeping at night. Is it a type of art? Animals? Herbs? Technology? Sport? What matters a lot to you in life? What are the things that make you lose track of time while doing or thinking about?

What are the things that, when you do them, you feel strong confidence and connection? What do you want to proudly leave behind you? What are the things that you are "willing to die for" as Moustafa Hamwi says? What are the things that you are willing to tolerate pain, criticism and setbacks for, as you cannot imagine your life without them? What makes you happy and brings stars to your eyes?

After feeling again those lovely sensations in your body and heart, think about what robbed this endless pleasure from your life? What were the social norms or parents' expectations that buried this magic deep inside you, until you lost touch with it and felt like you don't know it anymore? What was the external noise that has taken your attention away from what you truly love? And fooled you with the idea that you are doing great, while deep inside you are having a little voice screaming, "Get me out!".

Think about how you can reclaim this magic and put it into place. This passion could become a business that benefits others and brings you money. If so, great, but it doesn't need to be. When you are practising your passion on a daily basis, you are practising a huge amount of love towards yourself. And, again, you cannot love anyone else genuinely and congruently until you love yourself first.

We often feel handcuffed by fear. It could be fear of failure, taking the wrong decision, or letting go of the familiar. This may cause us to feel angry with people who remind us about our passion and purpose, even if they are doing it in the kindest way. Because it reminds us of our responsibility towards our own happiness. What we don't realize is that the moment we are congruent to ourselves and following our heart's calling, everything starts falling into place. Doors of opportunities start opening to us like magic.

What does pursuing our passion mean? It means taking relentless actions to go after it persistently and patiently, and never quitting it until it shines. We need at those moments to learn how to live an ordinary life, not thinking about gaining a lot of money.

When people are too concerned about money, they may choose to remain stuck at a job they hate, driving them ill due to excessive stress, and the money they get will be spent on curing their illness rather than enjoying their lives. So, rather than going through this painful cycle, we can enjoy our lives even with less money by practising what we love every day, which will bring us more energy, boost our immunity and prevent illness.

Some people play it safe and practise their passion after work or on weekends while holding a full-time job with constant income. From personal experience, I know that after working long hours doing something you hate, you get home feeling drained. It's hard to find the energy required to pursue your passion. Other times you may find energy practising your passion, only to go to work and lose it again. No energy is left for other activities in life. You get stuck in this closed loop of constant filling and immediate draining, without getting a chance to enjoy what you gain.

During weekends, you need to replenish your connections with family and friends in addition to practising your passion and resting. How balanced can your life be? I am not saying don't plan your transition. I am rather saying don't keep postponing taking action out of fear, because risk will always be there. You can get fired from your job at any time. Think carefully about it.

Exercise 3.1: Your Self-love Contract

This is a reality check exercise. You will discover how you have been jeopardizing your self-love and learn to take more loving choices instead. At the end of the exercise, you will sign your self-love contract, and take the pledge to live by it every single day.

Q1: What are the five most judgmental statements you tell yourself/others about yourself?
I am:

1. _____

2. _____

3. _____

4. _____

5. _____

Q2: What do you want to replace them with?
I am:

1. _____

2. _____

3. _____

4. _____

5. _____

Q3: What kind of negative self-talk have you programmed your mind with?
Example: It is difficult to succeed these days.

It's: _____

Life is: _____

I can't: _____

Q4: Knowing that we get what we believe, what do you want to believe instead?
Example: Everything comes to me easily.

Life is: _____

I can: _____

Self-love is: _____

Q5: How are you being judgmental to others?
Example: People are too strict.

_____

_____

Q6: What do you want to replace those thoughts with?

_____

_____

Q7: In what ways are you being unloving towards yourself?

_____

_____

Q8: What is the positive intention behind your behaviour towards yourself?

_____

_____

Q9: Your self-love contract:

Write down: I (your first and last names) love myself unconditionally, in all its parts, the ones I am aware of, and the ones I am not yet aware of. I promise to embark on a journey of self-discovery, self-love, and contentment every single day. I promise myself to do whatever it takes to reach the level of self-love that will bring me happiness, joy and satisfaction in the best way I can, every single day.

Signature: _____

Additional resources

♥ The following guided meditation will help you reclaim your passion and purpose. Do it every day, after waking up or before you sleep, to reinforce the idea in your mind, and create enough noise inside it, until you feel compelled to start practising what you are passionate about again. https://youtu.be/ukIqUEejx1g

If you are serious about your desire for a better life full of love, peace and fulfilment, then you need to alter the way you think about pain. Start taking uncomfortable actions to propel and sustain self-love. Choose carefully the places you go to, the things you do, and the people you spend time with. Change the situations and conditions you don't like. Voice your feelings, needs, and desires. And do whatever it takes to live your life freely and congruently.

Start a journey towards self-love. Assess the quality of your relationships and notice how you might be unconsciously applying love misconceptions in your life. Be willing to dive in, knowing that this inner journey will require a lot of effort and courage to see things about yourself that you haven't seen before. Activate your courage and change what requires changing.

Reclaim your lost passions and cultivate new ones. Live with your passion, love it and take action to pursue it, with tenacity and patience. Be willing to take criticism and setbacks yet get up again and continue your quest to live the life you want every single day.

Your passions fuel you. Love yourself enough to give it what brings it happiness and joy.

Make it a habit to listen to your heart. Check what it tells you about the people you spend your time with, the activities you do, and the choices and decisions you make. Are they loving enough, and do they work to your benefit in the long run? Or do they just bring you instantaneous gratification? Don't let love misconceptions fool you. Understand when there is an unhealthy pattern in your life and work to change it, either by yourself or by seeking help from an expert.

Think about your dreams and live them in your mind's eyes and your body's muscles. Feel them with your emotions for 10 minutes at least three times a day. Thank GOD for that feeling and for being able to see your dreams in your physical realm, even if it is still in your imagination. Because when you live with your dreams in your body, mind and heart, you will go out searching for ways to make them happen. Go out and pursue your passions patiently and persistently. And remember "When we are deeply connected to ourselves, following our passions and true callings in life, we don't just compete, we dominate".

Before moving to the next chapter, make sure to do all the exercises in this chapter and the previous chapters, more than once and with diligence, patience and compassion. Be positive about every single shift that you achieve along the way, even when you don't see immediate results in the physical realm. Believe that a shift is happening in your inner world; with persistent actions it will gradually manifest in your physical world. It will change your life into something you love.

Keep doing what you are doing with unwavering belief and in time you will certainly reap results. Test how practising the principles in this chapter make you feel. Do they bring you happiness and positive sensations in your body? In a moment I will tell you the story of Qabas Shaer and see how she turned the passion she discovered in adulthood into a successful business.

After becoming an enlightened soul that is vibrating with love and self-contentment, you are ready to move to the next level in life, creating healthy and happy connections with other people. Bear in mind that we are all different. You will need to accept these differences and perceive them as magnificent flavours that distinguish human beings from each other. This will help you approach inevitable conflicts with a more flexible mindset and seize them as opportunities to learn about others. These conflicts become the dream doors that you use to strengthen your relationships with others.

The Unspoken Magic of the Bricks

*"Everyone has their own destiny.
Not everyone makes the choice to pursue it."*

— ANONYMOUS

When I met Qabas Shaer in the LEGO Serious Play® sessions she offered at the Dubai Businesswomen Council, I felt intrigued by her passion for the bricks, and her professionalism in utilizing them to dig deeper into human minds and souls. This passion was so evident and contagious that I fell in love with the bricks myself. I started asking Qabas to use Lego over our coffee meetings, and to go together to the magical Lego Land in Dubai. And one day, it happened!

It was such an "Aha!" moment to see all of those amazing models created by thousands of tiny bricks, brick by brick. When I decided to write my book about loving and happy relationships, I couldn't leave out her story of love with those tiny, yet powerful pieces of art. When I asked Qabas what first attracted her to Lego and how her passion developed, she became nostalgic and started telling me her story of love.

Qabas was travelling with her family to a European country. She got up in the morning and was heading with them to the hotel's restaurant for breakfast when a small sign caught her sight. It was for a workshop taking place at one of the hotel's conference rooms. She felt an immediate force compelling her to follow the sign. In the conference room she saw something fascinating: a group of adults holding Lego bricks to build models. They were so attached to the bricks! Out of respect to their sacred moment, she refrained from opening the door and rather decided to ask the hotel management about the workshop.

Qabas felt those unusual events as a calling to her destiny. It was as if the bricks had come searching for her, to invite her to their world, so she decided to answer the call and took the LEGO Serious Playâ Facilitator workshop. It was about using the bricks as a tool for expression.

When she first touched them, she felt a sudden weight on her brain and emotions. What was she going to do with these tiny pieces?! How was she going to transform her thoughts into physical form? It was daunting to the mind because in this process the subconscious mind becomes the leader and gives signals to the hands to present the thoughts. As the subconscious mind represented by hands does not lie, and can't be manipulated, the person finds him or herself face to face with their reality. They can only see their truth.

Qabas started seeing the bricks as a channel or a pathway to release her inner thoughts and voices. Their ability to form bonds with each other was captivating. But there were also inner fears of change, of the unknown, of uncertainty. She had doubts about the success of this venture, especially that she was learning this method in a culture completely different from where she was intending to implement the idea.

She feared that this idea and her relationship to the bricks might not be appreciated in her work environment. But what if this was going to be her escape from the chains of the job she had at that time? She always had the dream of freeing herself, to do something creative, and different from the traditional training or consulting. Something she could find herself in. Qabas was about to change her career path until she met the bricks and the magic happened!

As time passed those fears transformed into different feelings. They became hope and excitement. She started seeing the bricks as her sanctuary to practise her silence, a place to be herself, and express herself freely, without any need to beautify her words or define their meanings. A place where no judgment, no rules, and no justifications were required.

Once she held the bricks, she felt like her whole brain was in her hands. The process engaged all her senses and energy to transfer what was in her heart, mind, and soul into the bricks. She states that initially the person feels heaviness and tiredness in the hands, because they are carrying the whole flow of energy of signals from the subconscious mind. The hands become trembling and electrified, as they carry the flow and blood circulation from the head and the heart.

Once the model is completed the eyes become dominant. They become magnified to embrace the output, to see the transformation of ideas and thoughts of the subconscious mind into the complete picture that the hands have made. The subconscious mind works mainly on details because it is based on instantaneous sparks or feelings, but the output is much bigger than those small details. It shows the whole picture, the complete story, which can only be defined by the conscious mind. The process becomes like drawing a painting with one touch of the brush at each moment or building the model brick by brick.

132

Qabas sees the bricks as a companion in thinking, explaining, and strategizing. They work like a bridge or a railway that connects people together and can accurately deliver our message to the audience. The language we usually speak and the words we use to express the inner voices might not be always accurate, causing the voices to lose part of their value, whereas the bricks transform those voices into something deeper before being spoken to the world.

A creative model from Qabas's workshops

SECTION 4

Connecting with Love

CHAPTER 4

Bridging with Love

Accepting others for who they are with all their parts and loving them as we love ourselves will create a happy, healthy and peaceful connection.

"I believe the greatest gift I can conceive of having from anyone is to be seen, heard, understood, and touched by them. And the greatest gift I can give is to see, hear, understand, and touch another person. When this is done, I feel contact has been made."

— VIRGINIA SATIR

When we build rigid rules about how we want people to be or act, we create a huge space of separation. Because people are human. They are instinctively different. When we expect them to be a second copy of us, in the way they talk, communicate, and connect, we are setting up ourselves for failure. We keep diminishing the other person's concept of self, and their feelings of self-worth, especially when we attach punishment to all their mistakes. This will cause people to start hiding what they feel, and their true self. And we end up walking in life like strangers.

Human beings can seem so mystic. Some people say what they feel freely and openly, while others are trained to hide their emotions; they can easily feel something and say the opposite. Some will ask a lot of questions out of interest yet be perceived as intimidating and criticizing. Some are compassionate and emotionally sensitive, while others are competitive and always want to win the game. These differences need to be recognized as bringing something new and unique to the world if we want to avoid a lot of tension between people.

By the end of this chapter, you will learn how to bridge to other people, despite all differences, with love and acceptance, respecting them for who they are, communicating openly and honestly to tackle inevitable conflicts more wisely, and using these conflicts as a dream door to learn more about the other person and establish a stronger and deeper connection.

Have you ever felt like you are saying one thing, but the other person is hearing something else? Are you tired of being misunderstood and feeling rejected, helpless and confused? I have been there, and many people have been there too. It becomes painful to the point where you feel like no matter what you say, the other person wants to misunderstand you! And when you clarify yourself, they tell you "but why didn't you say this before?"! This does not only happen in conversation; it can also happen in regard to our actions, or by simply living our lives as we are.

Why do you think this happens? Because people are conditioned by fear – fear of not being accepted for who they are, of being abandoned and losing their sense of belonging. This is rooted in the deepest fear of walking around with injured self-esteem. When our self-esteem or soul is wounded due to unhealthy communication, carelessness, and unconscious actions, our concept of self is destroyed, and we lose our power. We can't secure our basic needs in life, in turn affecting our survival on earth.

The pandemic of disconnection

Through the years people have learned to give away parts of themselves, one of which is their congruence. We see them wearing emotional and intellectual masks almost all the time. They feel one thing but say something else, think about one thing and do something different. What is worse, they are expected to do so, and when they start expressing their true thoughts and feelings freely and honestly, they are considered awkward and made to feel unwelcome – or it is used against them to make them ashamed.

The whole world is programmed to hide, to hide thoughts, feelings, and even the truth. We see strangers and mystery around us everywhere, starting with co-workers and schoolmates, and ending with friends, partners and family members. Everyone is becoming unknown and unpredictable; in many cases they are "unsafe zones" to go to with open mind and heart.

It is important to know that nobody was born this way. It wasn't printed on their genes to be dishonest and lack integrity. It is a learned behaviour, due to social conditioning about what is expected and accepted and what is not. It makes people cover themselves with hundreds of layers so that others don't know who they really are. They are scared to death that if they remove the cover, they will be hit in their core self-concept and self-worth.

It becomes a paradigm: even people craving the freedom to be who they really are following obediently. When they meet someone taking steps towards change, they pull him or her back. Yes, it is done unconsciously, but it occurs. The world is working against itself in an absurd manner. But the good news is that these learned behaviours can be unlearned once we become open to new possibilities and are willing to get out of our comfort zone and try something new.

We need to take persistent steps towards change, with a lot of compassion and patience. It all starts with the self. Massive change can happen in our lives when we start reclaiming the freedom to see and hear what is going on rather than what *should* be, the freedom to feel our feelings and express them congruently, the freedom to share our thoughts, ask for what we want without seeking permission, and take risks on our own behalf. We can start by taking baby steps and building on them as we move to bigger actions.

Creating connections

The first step to creating a connection is maintaining a physically open position during conversations. When people are facing each other, sitting closely, looking at each other in the eyes, and giving their full attention, the effect is completely different from being far away from each other, being busy doing something else, sitting while the other person is standing, or looking away while talking.

This step is crucial. It tells the other person that they matter and what they say is valuable. Whether the situation is a casual conversation between co-workers or a major conflict between a couple who are trying to resolve it, this setup helps in building intimacy.

The next step is focusing inwardly for a minute to explore what we are thinking or feeling and expressing these thoughts and emotions as they come, without fear of judgment or rejection. At this stage, the spoken words will craft the emotional bridge between people. It is important to ensure that all spoken words are preserving the worth of both the speaker and the listener. Because the moment self-worth is injured, the connection is lost.

We need at this stage to believe that we are whole and complete. We have the courage to explore the parts of ourselves that don't serve us anymore and replace them with more useful ones, while keeping those that are still working for us. We can make sense of people and the world around us, allowing them to be who they are without feeling offended. Most importantly, we know how to bridge with love and total acceptance of others and believe that we can do it.

Dealing with diversity

The differences between people are endless: physical appearance and capabilities, race, age, culture, religion, education, social conditions, preferences, etc. Differences are inevitable even between identical twins. What matters is dealing with them in a way that allows our relationships to flourish and thrive.

The secret lies in how we treat our feelings about ourselves and others. Do we reject them? Do we project them onto others? Do we pretend they don't exist? Do we suppress them, causing the emotional atmosphere to become agitated with feelings? Or do we express them freely and openly? And when we express our true feelings, are we communicating their true meaning congruently, with full respect to our self-esteem and the other person? Or is it done carelessly?

In addition to expressing our thoughts and emotions honestly, congruence also means being willing to deal with new situations, places, cultures, and people, even if it seems risky. In every situation, human beings want to matter, whether they say it boldly by words and actions or hide it inside. It is a matter of life or death to them. When people lack congruence in their communication, the situation becomes a win/lose, right/wrong, dominant/submissive play.

The question becomes "Who will have more power over the other?". This is the worst thing to do to our relationships if we want them to last and bring us happiness. Why not choose a different way to feel this power and sense of self-worth? Why not start exercising our freedom to feel, to see, to hear, to express, to be, and to take risks by trying new things and allowing others to do the same? It is possible, but only if we are willing to do it.

Conflicts are opportunities for growth

Conflicts are not bad things. It is rather our perception of them as being destructive that causes us to do our best to eliminate or avoid them. When we look at conflicts as opportunities to learn about ourselves and the people we are in relationships with, they become our dream doors to new possibilities; they take the relationship to levels and directions that we never expected or even imagined. As Virginia Satir said, "We get together on the basis of our similarities, and we grow on the basis of our differences".

It is those superficial differences that cause conflicts to happen. Once we dig down to our deepest desires in relationships, we find commonalities in people's dreams of being accepted, loved, and fulfilled. The most vital element of creating a connection is communication. The type of communication we habitually follow governs the type of connection we establish. This is where friction starts.

Frictions escalate, sometimes affecting people's health and ruining their relationships. We need to deal with friction wisely. If we want to overcome tough times in our relationships, rather than avoiding conflicts and considering them monsters, we can activate our emotional gauge, choose to learn about ourselves and others with an open mind and heart, and take intentional, loving, and peaceful actions to deepen the relationships.

If we are serious about resolving conflicts, we need to open the door for transparent discussions and express our authentic thoughts and feelings to people. A hotel once wrote a message for its clients on the wall saying, "If you like something, talk to people, and if you don't, talk to us!". Confrontation is not a bad thing, it gives you an opportunity to connect from the heart, express yourself, speak your mind, and ask for what you want.

When people with low self-worth communicate, even with the best intentions, they either attribute unintended meaning to what they hear, or they send their message in a way that does not allow the other person to perceive its true meaning. This affects the sender, the receiver and the relationship between them. Such people tend to follow one of these four unhealthy communication styles:

1. **Pleasing**: aiming to please others at the expense of their own dreams and desires, thinking that they must have done something wrong; this often causes them to experience chronic stomach pain.

2. **Blaming**: pointing fingers and making others responsible for their own feelings, which is associated with a lot of body tension.

3. **Avoiding**: shutting off communication by being super logical, focusing only on facts, ignoring their emotions and requesting the other person to do so, which is usually associated with feeling drained.

4. **Being chaotic**: talking about many unconnected topics, jumping from one to another to get the attention of the other person in any possible way, causing themselves and others to feel dizzy and off-balance.

People with low self-worth are usually scared and dependent on others for feeling alive. They use the above methods as defensive mechanisms, while inside they feel unworthy of the love they crave. But these coping mechanisms don't allow them to access their creative resources to communicate, connect, and bridge to others with love and acceptance.

It might be a relief to know that these forms of communication are universal, regardless of culture, age, and gender. We may all slip sometimes, but the important thing is to observe ourselves, pay attention to the way(s) of communication we tend to use during moments of weakness, and take an honest decision to slowly and patiently change them, as they simply don't serve us.

It is also necessary to know that the more we become emotionally dependent, the more life will distract people away from us, even if they don't want to do so. This happens to teach us a valuable lesson about the importance of being emotionally independent, of using our inner resources to empower us. Only then we can build healthy relationships with others, based on interdependent connections, where everyone is whole by himself or herself and willing to give as much as they receive.

The best way to communicate is to be congruent, with our words, feelings, body and facial expressions all aligned. We take actions based on this powerful alignment. This way our communication will be clear, easily understood, trusted, and believed. This power will help us access all our resources and find creative ways to create healthy and happy connections. It helps us to ease conflicts brought about by poor coping mechanisms and communication styles, to release physical pain and live a meaningful life with happiness and joy.

Exercise 4.1: Crafting your own kingdom

In this exercise you will define the characteristics, preferences, beliefs, rules, and social conditioning of your own kingdom. It is your land with its set boundaries that you carry everywhere you go. It governs how you behave in all relationships and what kind of people and situations you bring into your life:

1. Take an empty box that you love or buy a new one that appeals to you.

2. Go on a tour at your home and collect the things that speak to you. You can also use small pieces of paper to draw or write the names of things that represent something meaningful to you.

3. Give a name/title/description to each piece and put the collection in your box.

4. These could be the names of people you avoid or people you enjoy their company, with a description explaining why you feel this way about them.

5. They can also be hobbies and interests, or opinions about things, behaviours, attitudes, events, and places. Be wild and creative.

6. Make sure to include everything that evokes strong emotions, whether love, hate, anger, joy, disgust, fear, shame...etc.

7. This is your kingdom, the one that goes into the world with you. Parts of it are known to you and to others; other parts are hidden inside you, but they still govern your choices – about people and situations and how to interact in your relationships.

8. Keep your kingdom in a place where you can see it at least once a day for a few weeks, to remind you about your preferences and choices in life.

Exercise 4.2: The respectful passionate traveller

After defining your own land, you can travel to other people's lands for exploration:

1. Choose someone you want to create a connection with.
2. Do the previous exercise with them to learn about their lands and how they prefer people to enter them.
3. Teach them about yours in a very subtle and kind way.
4. Establish the physical positioning we spoke about in creating a healthy connection.
5. Start communicating by choosing the parts (topics/preferences) where you both meet first. Commonality will bring you closer.
6. Explore their strengths with curiosity and educate them about yours.
7. Find a way to make a more creative land that can fit both of you. Blend your strengths. This is the area where you can complement, teach and enrich each other's lives.
8. Ensure that you navigate through the process with total respect to their preferences, without losing yours. This can only be done by activating the gauge of your

emotions and expressing them as they come freely and congruently.

Exercise 4.3: Agree how to disagree

In this exercise you will decide how to communicate during conflicts. What are the expressions and words you love to hear, as they are associated with beautiful meanings to you, and what are the expressions and words to be avoided?

1. Get a large piece of white paper, A3 or bigger.
2. Ask the person you want to bridge to how to know when they are upset. Write it on the paper.
3. Ask yourself the same question and write the answer.
4. Ask the other person and yourself how you would like the other person to approach when you or they are feeling upset? Write it down.
5. As there are degrees to emotions (i.e., upset, disappointed, agitated, enraged...etc.), write down the preferable approaches to be used for both of you associated with each degree of the emotion (ex: When feeling upset do .... And if feeling enraged, then do....)
6. Write down any trigger words to be avoided.
7. Sign this agreement and ask the person to read it carefully and do the same.
8. Hang this contract in a place where both of you can refer to it while in conflict.
9. Put it into action once any conflict arises, no matter how big or small, and measure the effect.
10. If anything requires adjustment, do so and renew your signatures to the new contract.

Until and unless we are deeply connected to ourselves, honest about our thoughts and feelings, and are expressing them freely and congruently, we cannot create healthy connections with others. It starts with making healthy contact and bridging to the other person by seeing, hearing and loving them unconditionally. This means allowing them to be who they really are, to share with us their inner fruits and true selves. At the same time, we need to be totally in love with ourselves and show who we really are without shame or guilt.

When we live with integrity, we feel valued, become healthier, and are able to tackle anything that comes our way with wisdom. Not only that, but we are also able to enrich our lives with the blended strengths offered by the people around us. When we approach their lands with respect – entering them the way they prefer us to and inviting them to ours in a subtle welcoming way, without demanding or clinging – we create the chance for a new blended land to be formed, where we complement and elevate each other in the most loving way possible.

This requires a lot of patience. We are unlearning the social norms that became engraved on our minds, to the point that we are practising them unconsciously and sometimes blindly and starting to learn new ways. Learning is change. The natural process of change comes with a lot of uncertainty; it threatens our safety and moves us away from our known zones. That's why we need to be patient as we practise these learned concepts, both with ourselves and others.

I love to say that happy relationships don't just happen! We build and keep replenishing them all the time. By now you have learned that social pre-conditioning is what causes people to build walls to protect their self-esteem from being injured. In order to build happy and healthy relationships with others, we must first take care of our own self-worth in a kind way. Self-worth is the place from which we gain energy, feel safe, and approach life with full force. Then we connect to others in a way that protects their self-worth too.

You have also learned that all human beings are different, no matter how much their external conditions match. It is vital to treat these differences with full respect and acceptance. As an aid to doing this we need to explore our own lands with all their parts, and the lands of people around us, to invite them to our lands in the most welcoming way possible and visit their lands in ways they prefer. This is a lifelong process; it cannot be done with the press of a button. However, I promise that the more you practise it, the closer you get to what you want.

While building our bridges, we will slip into the inevitable conflicts at times. That is okay, as long as we choose to utilize these conflicts to learn about our own preferences and those of others. Adjust, and try building the bridge again. This time it will be much stronger.

If you skipped the first chapters and haven't done their exercises, I invite you to read them and do all their exercises now. This book is written in a structured manner to build a chain of love, where each step leads to the next. Once you are done, list all the relationships that you want to replenish or fix, write your aspirations about them, and then do the exercises in this chapter.

After that, write down the kind of changes you think are needed in the listed relationships, based on the information learned. Start with small things, do them repeatedly and monitor the difference. Don't stop until the newly learned ways become your new norm for bridging to others with love. Celebrate your winnings and do more of what worked. With time, patience and diligence a shift will happen, and you will have the enriched relationships you always wanted.

At the end of this chapter, I will share with you a story about how a beautiful soul rescued a lovely girl from being suicidal to becoming a successful photographer. This story will give a real example about how accepting others for who they are, treating them with kindness and respect, despite any problems they go through, or imperfections they have, will impact their whole lives.

This chapter was about building happy and healthy relationships with people in general. It leads us to the next step: building a loving and happy intimate relationship with the significant other. Such relationships are intricate, requiring more sensitivity and extra care due to the physical closeness partners reach. The kinds of goals couples want to achieve in life differ from the ones that people set for their general relationships.

Knight in Shining Armor

"Feelings of worth can flourish only in an atmosphere
where individual differences are appreciated,
mistakes are tolerated, communication is open,
and rules are flexible."

— VIRGINIA SATIR

I will tell you a story about a special and decent relationship. In it a respected friend played the role of a hero, a saviour, a knight in shining armor in his friend's life. A kind human who brought light to Marwa's life, giving her hope and a reason to live! Samer was teaching arts at the same college where Marwa studied, in Egypt. The first thing that caught Marwa's attention was Samer's looks. He was a handsome man, but she just watched him from a distance.

Marwa graduated and years passed by... She was dreaming about becoming a master in her field, and to do something that wasn't done before. To have her unique style in photography and become a successful photographer. She continued her journey of learning and searched for a long time to find a mentor to give her the guidance and knowledge she was craving, someone to teach her unique aspects of photography. One day, through social media, her wish was fulfilled.

Marwa had the habit of following artists of fine taste and was connected to all her schoolteachers on Facebook. At New

Year, she sent a personalized greeting to all her connections, including Samer, and the magic happened! He replied! They started chatting and exchanging messages until they became close friends. Samer mentioned to Marwa that he liked her posts, as they gave him hope and encouragement. At that time Marwa was trying to boost herself and others by sharing motivational posts on her profile. It seems that Samer was one of her loyal audience.

Samer had fine artistic taste and was advanced in his field of art, so he took the lead and started pushing her forward. He sensed her passion about photography and saw in her what others could not see. He believed that she could do something special and that meant a lot to her. Marwa believes that when you find someone who sees you from inside and believes in your potential, you can do miracles.

Marwa's life got busy and her contact with Samer decreased. She had some difficult experiences, causing her to go into depression and attempt suicide. Thank GOD someone found her at the right moment, and she was admitted to emergency. Marwa was in deep pain and felt darkness all around her. At that moment, her angel Samer showed up to give her light and encourage her to resume photography. She got enlightened and started shooting again. She took her shots from the heart. She did her best to impress him and show him that she was improving.

Samer gave Marwa her life back. He saw the gem inside Marwa and helped her to love herself more. He made her want to be in good shape, do more, be more, and make a dent in the world to prove to him that what he saw in her was real. His existence made her feel safe; he gave Marwa energy to keep going and keep achieving. Marwa called Samer her angel because she saw in him an angelic character who supports people, loves helping them, and always wanted the best for them.

At one point, Marwa started shifting her focus from herself to Samer's artistic taste and talent and was impressed by his success. She wanted to have a close look at his work and went to visit his gallery, which consisted of a small room and another bigger room filled with artistic tools and artwork. He played soft Western music in the background.

Marwa was like a kid who entered a candy shop! She kept looking at his amazing art filling the shelves and hanging in the ceiling with smiling eyes! It was like a different world to her! The world of dreams! The place was filled with the smell of colours and mud that he used for his work. The outer yard was filled with trees. It felt a very comfortable and quiet environment in which to work.

To visit someone who was so successful in his art meant a lot to Marwa. And what intrigued her the most was Samer's humility and simplicity despite his many travels and successes around the world. This encouraged her to show her natural self, without any formalities or ranking. She trusted sharing her secrets with him without fear of being judged.

Samer was a good listener; he would look straight in peoples' eyes and could sense their pain without them even talking about it. Despite this amazing experience, Marwa had a secret fear of losing Samer. She was afraid of becoming a burden to him as she is the kind of person who talks and shares a lot. She felt that she leaned a lot on him, which she saw as a selfish act because she was only complaining and never listened to his problems. It is true that he was her only trusted friend at that time and meant the world to her, but she got scared of becoming addicted to him, which is unhealthy. That's why she decided to let him go and distanced herself for a long time, despite his great positive impact on her life.

Marwa hasn't met Samer for a while now, and she hopes to meet him one day when she becomes very successful in her photography work. The last time they met she wasn't in very good shape physically or emotionally; she wishes when they meet again to proudly tell him that she has become successful in everything she is doing, and that she is very happy to meet him again.

Marwa is also intending to listen to him a lot, learn about his life, and share with him her new personality, success and transformational journey into the best version of herself. She will tell him that he was the sun that spread his light to the moon and lit her life with hope and happiness. Marwa dreams for this meeting to be a very special and unforgettable one, with lots of laughter and joy.

CHAPTER 5

The Happy Couple

When two ready souls meet and decide to connect with love, they spread the ripple of happiness, and conquer the world together.

"Love is a game that two can play, and both win."

— EVA GABOR

We see a lot of loneliness and separation between married couples nowadays. Even couples who choose to stay together and avoid divorce, are living as two separate and empty souls. This makes us wonder if having a loving, happy and healthy intimate relationship is possible. A wise way to handle such a puzzling phenomenon is by asking the question "How can we make such a relationship possible?" The answer is "When two ready souls meet, the flame of love kindles, and they take the pledge to keep replenishing it along the way".

I believe that any hurdle in life can be overcome by more love and compassion. The more love we have, the more peace we can spread to the world. By the end of this chapter, you will be able to learn the secret behind spiritual separation despite physical connectedness. You will understand the extra sensitivity surrounding intimate relationships. You will know when it is the right time to meet your soulmate, how to know him/her, how to express your feelings in a meaningful and loving way, how to flip the death dance into a loving tango, and when conflicts escalate, how to ride your relationship horse without breaking it.

You will understand that the first key to building a happy and healthy relationship is to be connected to yourself, to show love, care, compassion and acceptance to yourself in a way that speaks to you. The second key is being honest about what is going on inside you (i.e., your thoughts and emotions), and choosing to communicate it congruently, without jeopardizing your self-esteem or affecting the self-worth of your partner. Because when self-worth gets injured, connection is lost, resulting in unhappy and unhealthy relationships.

In January 2020 I ran a survey to understand the challenges that face couples in the first three years of marriage. I analysed the answers of more than 60 participants (men and women from different cultures and ages). The challenges were many and included not knowing each other in advance, dealing with differences, different communication styles, lack of unconditional love based on trust and respect, fear of repeating unsuccessful experiences, not expressing emotions freely and openly, change, lack of awareness of the responsibilities and roles of marriage, unrealistic expectations and the shock of reality, interference by in-laws, and financial issues.

All those difficulties cause couples to be unable to connect, leading them to a sense of separation, loneliness and emptiness in their relationship. Passion starts fading away and at some point, divorce may happen. I thought to myself "If we can tackle these issues before they arise and even before people get married, we can save couples a lot of troubles, by preventing them from feeling lonely, sad, scared, and confused. Even if we cannot eliminate these feelings completely, we can strive to reduce them tremendously". We will tackle some of the issues in this chapter, which looks at couples meeting to form the bond of love. The remaining issues will be discussed in the next chapter, when they start forming families and raising their kids together.

Meeting your soulmate

Many people spend more time and expenses planning for their wedding ceremony than preparing themselves to live beyond it. They often get married without defining their emotional and intellectual goals, or the needs and desires to be met in their marriage. Oftentimes they don't even know on a deep level why they are marrying the people they marry; they end up feeling hurt, heartbroken and living in severe pain. They meet someone they like and start thinking, "Oh, she is beautiful; he is successful; she cooks well; he is educated; she exercises... etc". Attraction grows into infatuation, and before they know it, they are married and hoping it is going to be a "happily ever after" story. There is nothing wrong with being attracted to someone's traits, but in the process of infatuation, people tend to overlook many important aspects, such as:

♥ Are they emotionally ready to build a relationship that will require them to open up their hearts to send and receive love?

Or are they still carrying pain from previous relationships and past experiences, causing them to close their hearts?

- Are they choosing because they really like the person, or is it a reaction to things they did not like in their previous relationships?
- Are they willing to work on themselves to release their old baggage?
- Are they able to be themselves with this person without fear of being judged?
- Do they feel safe and welcome in his/her existence? How does the other person treat them?
- How do they treat the other person? How does s/he feel in their existence?
- How willing are they to do whatever it takes to make this marriage work?

Sounds different from the rules people usually give for making the right choices, right? I know that you are expecting me to give you a standard recipe to choose the right partner. I am sorry to tell you there is no criterion that fits all. It is you who decide what right means to you, as long as you answer the above questions first. And before looking for the right partner, we need to ensure that we are the right partner too. We need to free ourselves from old rules and past experiences.

We know that we have achieved this when we start talking about the lessons learned from past experiences without emotional attachment to the painful parts. We have cultivated inner love and can show it to ourselves in whatever situation we are in. We can express our thoughts and feelings freely and can encourage the other person to do the same, regardless of their physical closeness or the amount of time we spend together. Only then can we say that we are ready to form a healthy and happy intimate relationship.

Once we live in this state of self-love and inner peace, we will notice people who are living in a similar mental and emotional state. We will be able to choose a partner whose state matches ours. This is the time to define what we want in an intimate relationship. Later in this chapter I will share an exercise to develop your relationship vision board, which will bring you more clarity when it comes to choosing the right partner for you.

Sometimes the right match is someone you show the least interest in, while deep inside your heart knows it is the person you need to be with for your growth in life. Trust what your heart tells you. I am not saying this to urge you to go after everyone who shows interest. I am rather suggesting paying attention to the wired internal attraction that you don't understand and listening to your inner whisper.

But before getting emotionally involved, and infatuation develops, you need to dig deeper for more exploration. You need to see if this person is someone you want to grow with emotionally, intellectually, physically and spiritually for a lifetime.

Love and be loved freely

Expressing our thoughts and emotions freely and congruently is part of our emotional readiness and continuous growth, and of having a relationship that sings. This happens when we are deeply in touch with our triggers, giving ourselves the permission to feel our feelings (despite any rules we had about them while growing up), and communicating them without shame or guilt. We know that we are congruent when we speak our thoughts and emotions without painful sensations in the stomach or choking in the throat.

According to Gary Chapman, people use five different languages to express or perceive love. These languages are:
I.   Words of affirmation, gratitude, and encouragement
II. Spending quality time doing something together with undivided attention
III. Acts of service, like helping in the household
IV. Physical touch, such as hugging and being close
V.   Offering gifts even if only a flower from the garden.

The concept behind the five languages of love comes from individual emotional tanks that need to be filled. These emotional tanks consist of five compartments, each of which occupies a different portion/percentage of the total tank. The combination of these portions differs from one person to another. Everyone has developed a tendency since childhood to respond to one of the languages more than the others to fill his/her tank, as it occupies the biggest portion. Problems arise when couples are seeking ways to MAKE the other person offer them something in their own way and talk their language, rather than taking the initiative to learn and speak their language of love. This explains why many spouses suffer from emotional hunger, tending to satisfy it through different types of addiction, to food, sweets, shopping, movies, work, drugs, … etc.

To overcome this challenge, we need to utilize curiosity and exploration of our partners' inner worlds, showing understanding and respect to what is going on inside them. Defining our preferred language of love saves us from misinterpreting simple actions as being mean or unloving. It will also save us from having the continuous pain of rejection. I suggest utilizing the concept of competition to see who is taking the initiative to get closer than the other. Who is supporting the other more? Let it come only from a place of love, free from any pride.

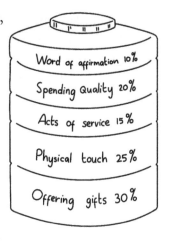

Let's say you expressed love towards your partner and his/her response was "don't just tell me you love me, do something". You may feel taken aback by the comment. But I encourage you before thinking they are rejecting you, to listen carefully to the yearning behind their complaint. They are telling you valuable information and are unconsciously teaching you about their language, what love means to them, and how they prefer to express and receive it. Take it as feedback, and next time try something from the love language "acts of service". Then see what their reaction will be.

It is important to know that people have different values, eliciting specific emotions. If you speak your partner's language of love but implement it in a way that comes with a cost to your or their values, you will not be satisfied or fulfilled. Something will always be missing in the relationship (your or their dignity/

self-worth), causing love to vanish with time. Learn about your partner's values, educate them about yours, and follow mutual understanding and respect. Doing these things will help you sustain your intimate love with the least effort and conflict possible.

The co-dependency-narcissistic death dance

People have different attachment styles in their relationships. Some of them are unhealthy attachments reflecting traumatic experiences from childhood and affecting their level of self-love. A common tragic example is the co-dependent-narcissist blend, which I call the "death dance".

Narcissism is defined as a personality disorder or mental condition in which a person has an inflated sense of importance, a deep need for excessive attention and admiration, troubled relationships, and a lack of empathy for others. Co-dependency is defined as high self-sacrifice, a focus on others' needs, suppression of one's own emotions, and attempts to control or fix other peoples' problems.

In my opinion, both traits result from being love deprived. It might appear more clearly with co-dependency than narcissism. But the root cause is the same in both. Co-dependent people dismiss their desires, wants and needs for the sake of fixing others. They think that by doing this they will gain importance, improve their self-worth, and hence be loved. What they don't know is they are trading their whole lives to get love in return. They have built an inner belief that they are not worthy of love and always have to pay a price to get it. Their emotional tanks are always empty, and they are continuously turning "outwards", seeking love and approval rather than turning "inwards" to feel them.

When someone does not have empathy towards other people, as in the case of narcissism, it only reflects their inability to have empathy towards themselves. As Dr Barbra De Angelis said, "All relationships are our mirrors, and all people are our teachers". And a person who does not have empathy towards himself/herself is absolutely lacking self-love. Coming from this severe emptiness inside, they tend to fill their emotional tanks from outside by demanding excessive attention and admiration, often in an aggressive way.

You may wonder how narcissists can have an inflated sense of importance and lack self-love. The answer is that it is a mask they wear to get other people's attention, which gives them the self-satisfaction they need. They are willing to do anything so that this mask does not go away. For them the attention they get fills their empty tank with love. As co-dependents tend to give a lot and get too little, they form a perfect blend with narcissists who will take a lot without feeling enough or giving anything in return.

Every human being has needs and desires to be fulfilled in order to reach equilibrium or a balanced state. And everyone chooses a different way to fulfil those needs. For narcissists it comes from having people in need of their approval or help so that they feel important and loved. It does not mean they will give them this approval, but they will be able to feed on their energy while these pleasers are seeking it. For co-dependents, it comes from having someone to fix, give excessive attention to, or pay the price of love to in advance, hoping that they will get this love in the form of help, affirmation or approval.

In time the co-dependent will feel exhausted and abused, and demand getting the love they paid for, but their demands are never fulfilled. They may take a courageous decision to leave, but the narcissist will make it great torture, as s/he is losing their mine of loving emotions. When one of them (either the narcissist or co-dependent) loses this delusion of love, s/he experiences a void and hurry to fill it in the only way they know – by finding another person with whom they can practise the same behaviours to elicit the same results.

Both go endlessly along in this cycle of "addictive relationships", which they think is benefiting them, but it never does. Once they develop awareness in every cell of their bodies and decide to break free from this cycle of addiction (by looking for love inwardly rather than from the outside), a shift starts happening. And they see real changes in their lives.

Riding your relationship horse without breaking it

There is a notion saying, "hurt people hurt people". It means that people who feel hurt have a tendency to hurt others, because it is all they know. They don't have anything else to give, neither to themselves nor to others. We have learned that the most devastating type of hurt is to our self-worth, because it is the core that people rely on for their survival. Hurt people have been hit a lot in their core, causing them to develop poor coping mechanisms to protect their existence. These mechanisms manifest in one of the following four poisonous behaviours. These behaviours pull us away from being congruent, towards a vague zone full of loneliness, sadness, and confusion, which adversely affects our health.

A. **Blaming**: an aggressive attack towards a person. Usually it starts with the word "you" followed by a title or generalized action such as "are lazy, always late, do nothing…". It is a kind of bullying to the partner. If you notice yourself in a pattern of blaming, it is better to replace it with other healthy behaviours as indicated in the table below. And when you are blamed, you can do things to ease the effect.

When you are blaming, do this instead:	When you get blamed, do this:
• Complain about a specific **behaviour** instead of using a generalized title.	• Think about the positive intention of the person who is blaming, understanding that they might be feeling hurt but don't know how to express themselves in a healthy way. Bring this to their attention and support them to change for the sake of the relationship.
• Talk about your feelings using the word "I" and then express your needs.	
• Focus on "what does the relationship need" instead of "who is doing what to whom".	

B. **Defensiveness**: this behaviour goes hand in hand with blaming. It is like a football game; the first team attacks and the other defends. They may also take the ball and turn back to attack the first team to win. This behaviour does not do any good to the couple or their relationship. The defensive person will always feel oppressed and the other will never learn to take responsibility for their mistakes. The relationship loses its balance.

When you are being defensive, do this instead:	When your partner is defensive, do this:
• Admit the mistake.	• Ask them what they heard you saying and if they felt attacked, rephrase your statement and say it differently to deliver your message.

When you are being defensive, do this instead:	When your partner is defensive, do this:
• Apologize.	• Assure your partner that you are not blaming them, nor you will take your love away if they make a mistake. There is rather a need that you have and want it to be fulfilled.
• Take responsibility to do the required actions.	• Seize this opportunity to learn about your partner and teach them about you, to take your relationship to a deeper bond.

C. **Contempt**: this behaviour is entangled with long term excessive negative thoughts about the partner and attempts to demean, undermine and disrespect them by any means. It is more aggressive than blaming because it destroys self-worth. It is the most poisonous behaviour, damaging the immune system of both the victim and the predator. Both become prone to illness, and it can definitely lead to divorce if not eliminated or reduced drastically.

When you are being contemptuous, do this instead:	When your partner is being contemptuous, do this:
• Remind yourself about good qualities in your partner and their contribution to the relationship day after day.	• Ask what the intention is behind what they are saying. Maybe they didn't mean to be contemptuous.

When you are being contemptuous, do this instead:	When your partner is being contemptuous, do this:
• Explain to your partner that you have long-term suppressed feelings and start expressing them freely and honestly using the words "I feel…".	• Ask if the person is aware of the impact of his/her behaviour on you and clarify if it's the impact s/he wanted to have. S/he might be using contempt unconsciously as they don't know a better way.
• Seek your partner's help as you regain your natural self. Tell them that you want to treat them with the respect they deserve, and you need their support with this.	
• Write down all the cynical and sarcastic words that you catch yourself using on a paper and hang them somewhere with a sign to eliminate them from your talk.	

D. **Stonewalling**: is a result of feeling flooded in a relationship, usually due to experiencing one or all of the previous poisonous behaviours for a long time. The partner starts tuning out or getting obsessively busy to avoid conversation. It can take an active form when they leave home or remain silent, or a passive form when they keep saying yes, ok, aha…etc. and do nothing about what they promised.

When you are stonewalling your partner, do this instead:	When your partner stonewalls you, do this:
• Inform your partner clearly and take time out to do something you love in order to soothe yourself, then get back to the conversation. When this type of behaviour persists, it can be as damaging to the relationship as the others.	• Self-soothe through meditation or relaxation practice.
• Understand the difference between the discomfort you feel and your imagination about the danger that may take place if you speak.	• Talk to your partner about the effect of their behaviour on you. Ask them if they are feeling flooded due to something you have done.
• Discuss your fears of conversing with your partner and set some healthy boundaries.	

Riding the horse of your relationship and handling tough conversations can always be done in a safe way if you bring more love and understanding to yourself, your partner, the relationship, and the whole situation around it.

Tango with love

> *"Couples often ignore each other's emotional needs*
> *out of mindlessness, not malice."*

— DR JOHN GOTTMAN

Every human being has the capacity to love and be loved, and every situation has the potential to be healed with more love and unconditional acceptance. This can happen when we assume a positive intention to human behaviours without judgements. Human reactions mostly result from the interpretation of an event and the meaning they attach to it, not the event itself or what is actually happening. We can see this when two people react to the same words or event differently.

We all have different brain receptors and mental processes; they send certain messages based on our past experiences. If we are disappointed by a person for long enough, we might decide "this person is not trustworthy and anything that comes from him/her is a lie". When we are born, we do not know much about the world around us. People feed us with information from their own experiences and their ideas about them.

If certain events we experience are intensely painful, they are associated in the memory with the emotions of fear or pain. We then interpret similar events as something unwelcome. When such events are repeatedly associated with certain people, these people become unwelcome too! In NLP this phenomenon is called "anchoring". When we anchor events, people, behaviours and places to certain emotions, like anger or pain, they become emotional triggers that work beyond our control.

It's very important to understand that I am not condoning toxic behaviours some people choose to follow. I am rather saying that many actions can be done with good intention but be perceived as the opposite. This is what can happen between couples in normal, non-abusive and non-toxic relationships, when the two speak different languages of love, or when they are perceived as blaming or attacking while they were actually trying to protect their partners from harm.

That's why it is important to communicate your messages directly and clearly. Distorted messages are vague in meaning. They confuse the partner, who will not be able to respond to the required need because s/he does not know what it is. Develop a "conflict agreement" in which both of you agree how to disagree. How do you want your partner to tell you they are upset about something you did? How do you want to approach it? How do you want to express your unhappiness to them? And how will they know it? When these things are defined in advance, they become a handy reference to return to whenever required.

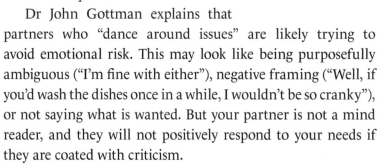

Dr John Gottman explains that partners who "dance around issues" are likely trying to avoid emotional risk. This may look like being purposefully ambiguous ("I'm fine with either"), negative framing ("Well, if you'd wash the dishes once in a while, I wouldn't be so cranky"), or not saying what is wanted. But your partner is not a mind reader, and they will not positively respond to your needs if they are coated with criticism.

While you may think you are playing it safe and avoiding conflicts by being indirect, this may increase the chances that you will be unsatisfied and that your partner will respond with resentment, causing the gap between you to increase. You were born with the freedom to rock the boat and express your needs in a relationship in more direct and loving ways, so reclaim that freedom and go for it. It will do wonders for your relationship and make it flourish in ways beyond your imagination.

You also need to stand up for what the relationship needs from both of you during a conflict. This will help you take the favour of both of you together and not one of you over the other. Allow yourself to use conflicts as an invitation for growth. There will always be an internal battle in which you fight two desires coming out of love, the desire to be more loving towards yourself and the desire to see your partner happy.

Embracing this fact will shift your focus from being defensive and resentful about what the other person wants from you, to your internal fighting desires and exploring a way to achieve a balance between them. This will help you to feel and act differently. Because when you choose to do something to see your partner happy, you will come from a strong place, as you are compromising to show your partner how much you love them and care about their happiness, and you are choosing to love over war. It's not because you are weak or unable to defend yourself.

A lady who was upset by her husband started talking about what she was going to do to get back at him. I felt intrigued and said to her, "Can you stop for a moment before acting and ask yourself why are you going to do these things? Are they coming from a place of hatred, to teach him a lesson, or are they are coming from a place of love?". She paused for few seconds and said, "You are right! It all comes back to the intention". That was all I wanted her to do, to ponder on her intentions.

Whenever you interact, ask yourself, "is this action coming out of love or out of fear and pain?". If it is fear, then it is coming from a reactive mood, not based on wisdom and what is best for the relationship to flourish. Fear comes from lack of self-trust that you'll be able to handle the situation no matter what happens, and lack of trust in GOD that he'll help and guide you along the way, and facilitate the best choices, ways and situations for you. Take intentional actions to show more love towards yourself and your partner and bring more love to the whole situation.

Exercise 5.1: Your relationship vision board

This exercise will help you explore what is important to you in a relationship and define what a happy and healthy relationship looks like to you. How do you express love and want to receive it? When will you say that the other person loves you? What do they need to say or do? Define your last frontier in a relationship: what do you have zero tolerance for that will break a relationship? What, in your own words, is the definition of love?
1. Prepare yourself to be without distraction for one hour.
2. Ensure the lighting is good, you are seated in a comfortable position, and your internal and external states are calm yet enthusiastic.
3. Using a paper and a pen, write anything that comes to your mind when you hear the words:
    - ♥ Love
    - ♥ Relationship
    - ♥ Marriage
    - ♥ Happiness
    - ♥ Friendship
    - ♥ Husband/Wife
    - ♥ Kids
    - ♥ Values

- ♥ Last frontiers
- ♥ A must have
- ♥ Intimacy
- ♥ Passion.

4. Start surfing the internet and search for the words that you put on paper.
5. Collect images that appeal to you and you think are relevant to these words and save them in a specific folder.
6. Once you are done, use an app on your mobile or a free site like picmonkey.com or canva.com for creating a collage.
7. Combine your collected images in a way that appeals to you.
8. Print the resulting collage and hang it in a place where you can see it multiple times every day, to remind you about what you want in your intimate relationship.
9. Whenever you meet someone you think will be a great match, come back to your vision board at a very early stage. This will help you to say yes or no, or to realize there are things to be discussed and negotiated before getting emotionally involved and experiencing infatuation blindness.

Exercise 5.2: Co-dependent-Narcissistic death dance healing strategy

This strategy is designed to help you understand the co-dependency-narcissism addictive relationship cycle that you might be trapped in, and help you break free of it.

Step 1: Acknowledge the situation by writing down the traits of people you are attracted to and examining the common ones. Are they needy/demanding? Are they controlling? Do they remind you of people or situations from your childhood?

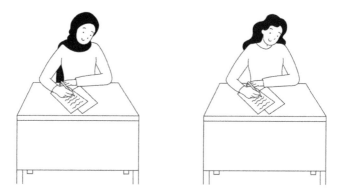

Step 2: Get help from a professional. When emotions are intense it is risky to tap into old wounds alone and without proper support. The journey of transformation will feel lonely and might throw you into a deeper depressive mood.

Step 3: Make this healing a priority and put yourself first. Understand that people who benefit from the old situation will do their best to resist the change in you and pull you back. Stand firm in your position and insist on bringing yourself out of this destructive cycle.

Step 4: Get support from compassionate friends and family members. During the first stages of change you will need a lot of encouragement and approval from people who know you outside the therapy/healing room, who know about your situation, and want you to have a better life. This kind

of emotional support along the way is crucial; it gives you affirmation and helps you celebrate your achievements.

Step 5: Join a 12-step relationship addiction-recovery group. If you can't find one nearby, establish one and invite people to it. These groups will give you a sense of normality as you are introduced to other people having the same problem. You will get a chance to listen to their stories, learn from them, and give and receive support and understanding from people who know how it feels to survive such circumstances. They understand it in their minds and feel it in their bodies and hearts.

Step 6: Do activities to nourish your mind, body, soul and heart. Exercise, eat healthy foods, practise mindfulness to help you be present and focused on the here and now, rather than reliving the painful past or feeling anxious about the unknown future.

Step 7: Be cautious about abuse attempts or manipulation from others. Don't hesitate to eliminate those people from your life and walk away. It could be an old friend who is not welcoming your change, an acquaintance who does not care about your feelings, or a taker who does not know how to give. Eliminating them will make a room for people with better behaviour to step in and give you love.

Step 8: Share your learning with others and celebrate your achievements as you progress along the way.

Exercise 5.3: *Love conversations*

Love conversations are meant to focus consistently on the things that you love in your partner and to express appreciation to him/her for having them. This will direct you focus to be on your partner's positive traits more and more. Your thoughts about their negative traits will shrink gradually, until they become insignificant and have minimal effect on your relationship.

1. Sit or stand on the same level as your partner, looking at them in the eyes.
2. Soften your gaze and start by telling them "I love you, (their name). I really do".
3. I love your…. Name all the personal, physical, emotional, and intellectual traits that you love and appreciate. Search and dig deeper. I am sure you'll find something, and rest assured that you'll get appreciation in return.
4. Let them say "I know, thank you!".
5. Give them a turn to show love and appreciation to you in the same way.
6. Tell them "I know, thank you!".

7. Repeat steps 3–6 as many times as you want, until both of you feel inner joy.
8. Let both of you feel and drink the love of the other person deeply inside and keep giving love in return.

9. Imagine your love tank getting filled higher and higher. If you notice that you need to receive love in another form, like a touch or a gift, state that in a positive way by saying "I feel very happy in your existence and my happiness will double if I get a small gift, a touch, help in..." whatever it is that you want.
10. Make the exercise as long as you want and repeat it at least once every week.

Exercise 5.4: Dealing with differences

This exercise will help you to deal with differences in background, culture, thinking, habits, beliefs, interests, lifestyle...etc. It will help you treat them with respect, giving the space for your partner to express himself/herself freely without being criticized, blamed or ashamed of who they are. It will greatly increase the safety zone between you and deepen the bond of trust.

1. Draw a big circle on the ground, using ropes, laces, toys, papers ... anything you find handy and feel comfortable with.
2. Put your name on a piece of paper and place it inside the circle. You may give yourself a funny nickname if you like, or one that represents something you are proud of.

3. Draw another circle for your partner or let them help you in drawing theirs. Put their name or nickname (if they choose one) inside their circle.

4. Fill your circle with everything that you feel is important to you, including your values, likes, dislikes, preferred language of love, words that trigger you positively or negatively, anything that will make this place signify your inner and outer worlds.

5. Let your partner do the same in their circle.

6. Give them an invitation card to your world. This could be something like "I am honoured to invite you, my beloved, to my special world. I will be happy when you come wearing these kinds of clothes, taking these actions, and saying these words (or any other variation that you prefer)".

7. Let your partner do the same.

8. Ensure to visit each other's world with a mind open to learning with respect. No titles or perceptions: just total acceptance for who they are with their differences. Remember that they don't have to be a copy of you for you to love or accept them. At these moments leave judgment, opinions and advices aside. It is not time for them.

9. If you find it hard to be in their world, with all its differences, don't worry; this exercise will help you to blend safely and create something magnificent. Take a step back to your world. Stay there for a few moments to rest and try again.

10. Get a hat and a basket. Call them "my curious exploratory gadget". Wear the hat and fill the basket with everything you saw and did not like in their world on small pieces of paper. Put the basket outside both worlds.

11. Use curiosity and ask questions as if you really don't know this person (even if you think you have known them for a long time).

12. Do your best to follow the things they like in their world and avoid what they don't like.

13. Repeat this exercise every two weeks or once a month. With time and repetition, you will get better at it and your relationship will become stronger. Differences will dissolve in their own way.

14. Have fun and be patient with yourself and your partner as well. Bring to the situation much love.

If you really want to meet the right soulmate and bond with love, you need to be a ready soul first. By ready I mean a person who is exercising unconditional love, compassion, acceptance and appreciation towards themselves. You are committed to your emotional, mental, physical and spiritual growth, communicating openly and honestly, and taking the responsibility to do whatever it takes to keep the flame of love in your intimate relationship alive.

It is not enough to be a ready soul and meet a ready one for your relationship to flourish. You need to learn about your soulmate, speak their language of love and teach them about yours. You need to express your feelings honestly and congruently and give your partner the space to do the same without judgments or criticism. You need to learn to ride the horse of your relationship without breaking it and avoid leaping into poisonous behaviours out of fear or when you feel your self-esteem is wounded. Turn your dependent love in the co-dependent-narcissism attachment into an interdependent love, where both are able to bring the best of themselves to the relationship, to tango with love. When you do this, no differences or conditions can affect your love or step in its way.

Oftentimes people make quick decisions based on instant attraction, before knowing the person well or even having an honest look in the mirror to see if they are ready to build a healthy and happy relationship with another human being. By now you know that this may lead to suffering and separation. It is better to work diligently on yourself, to become a ready soul first and make decisions based on what is right for you in the long run. Marriage is a continuous dance that we need to master.

You now also know that for a relationship to remain loving and healthy, we need to fill the emotional tank of our partners in the way they prefer, not in our way, and do it every single day. We need to be respectful travellers to their worlds, taking a journey of exploration of the self, learning about our partner and teaching them about us in a way that maintains their self-esteem and our own. This work may take time and effort to develop awareness and wisdom, but the sustained flame of love is definitely worth it.

Be aware not to slip into the dependent love patterns that lead us to make the wrong choices. Sometimes, even if we choose the right partners, they will get overwhelmed by behaviours originating from craving for love. This can be avoided when we feel secure, happy and whole by ourselves, when we connect out of desire rather than need. It is also important to remain kind during conflicts and avoid breaking the horses of our relationships. We do this by choosing loving acts rather than those coming from pain or a desire to win over the other person.

Promise yourself to live with the belief that having a miraculous loving relationship is possible because miracles do happen all the time. Be open and receptive to them. And when they happen, decide every day to bring more love and peace to yourself, your partner and your relationship. Manage your expectations from yourself and your partner by understanding your humanness, communicating your emotions freely and honestly, and appreciating any small progress you both make along the way.

When you know how to love yourself in the way your spirit craves, you take actions to satisfy this need and can make a pledge to connect to another ready soul with unconditional love and acceptance. The impossible becomes possible, and your ripple of love keeps multiplying.

After becoming a ready soul to form a healthy and happy intimate relationship, bonded with love to your soulmate, you are ready to build a healthy and happy family. You will learn in the next chapter how to build this family (your new-born system) and raise your children with love. You will be armed with the necessary tools and information, to bring them up in a psychologically healthy way, and send them to spread love and peace to the world.

Love Always Wins...

"I've loved you for a thousand years,
And I'll love you for a thousand more."

— Anonymous

I used to believe that love at first sight, leading to a long-lasting intimate relationship, was a fable, something we only see in movies. Then I came across this lovely couple who have been happily married for 47 years. It started when Alta met Nico Pretorius at a mutual friend's wedding in a neighbouring town. Alta was an angelic soul and a beautiful woman, and Nico was a handsome and affectionate army officer. His work had made him a very strict and precise person. Yet this did not stop his heart from dancing as he stood beside the groom, as the groom's man, and saw Alta's charming face, as she stood in her place as the maid of honour.

Their eyes locked and their souls recognized a familiar connection, as if they had an agreement to come to earth and live together the most wonderful love story ever. Each soul seemed to say, "I know you...and I miss you my soulmate... even though I don't recall meeting you in this physical form before...I have been searching for you...and now I have found you!".

They were officially introduced to each other at the wedding party and had the chance to get to know each other.

It was meant for this amazing seed of love to find its way when Alta missed her arranged transportation to get home, and the generous gentleman Nico offered her a drive. Alta took the call happily and they left the wedding early. But rather than going home, they went to see a movie together to lengthen the period of their connection and deepen their love. From those moments their love story grew bigger and became stronger.

Nico and Alta got married and lived in a modest caravan. As in any marriage, after the honeymoon came the salt. We all have the choice of how to use this salt. We can choose to use it to strengthen our love and deepen our relationship, or we can choose to allow its sharp taste to overcome the happy moments in life. Alta and Nico made the wise choice to use this salt to show how committed they were to the success of their marriage, how honest in their feelings they were, and how unique their love story was.

After six weeks of marriage, Nico went back to his duties in the army. He was keen to succeed in his career, to set an example for his children, support his family, and bring pride to his lovely woman. He worked hard, took many courses, attended training and had to sacrifice time with family. He missed them many days and nights but kept thinking about his beloved Alta and his three gorgeous daughters, who were as adorable as their mother, when he had to be away from them. This helped him replenish his love to them as he stayed connected to them by mind and heart. It continued for 30 years of his marriage.

The beautiful delicate flower, Alta Pretorius, who was considered an angel walking amongst humans, stayed as a silent and graceful rock to her family and sustained her inner strength despite her femininity and delicacy. She carried the responsibility of being a mother and a father for her daughters many days and nights, with full grace and love. She would always be there for them no matter how hard the situation was or how heavy the emotions were. Nothing ever looked too big or seemed too early or too late for her; she would sprinkle faith and hope amongst all her family members and do all that she could to support them practically, emotionally and spiritually. Alta took the decision to always be the glow of happiness to all her beloved.

Years passed by... Nico and Alta's love story survived many financial and social difficulties. When two of their adorable daughters got divorced, the pair experienced fear about how this might affect the grandchildren. But Love always wins! With more love they could sustain their happiness and prosperity, create an example for the generations to come, and grow their marriage into a deeper and stronger one. They became not only lovers or marriage partners, but also friends who adore each other and treasure their relationship. Their strong faith played a vital role in sustaining their happy marriage. And whenever a difficulty arose, their rule was to work as a team in their room away from children, talking softly, and never to go to bed angry.

One day Nico picked his daughter up from school, which was four hours away from their home, and took her for dinner. As a military man, Nico was usually strict and his daughters feared him, however, during this dinner he did something that changed his daughter's perspective about him for a lifetime. He started talking about his beloved Alta. As he talked about her, his heart opened completely, allowing his daughter to see a very soft and beautiful part of him and she danced with joy.

GOD rewarded Nico and Alta for their patience. He rekindled the heart of one of the divorced daughters with love again. She met a generous man who decided to build a new family with her and his four kids from a previous marriage. They united together with the blessings of the parents, and the joy of the whole family.

Nico is now a retired army General and a grandfather to 10 kids, six by birth and four bonus grandchildren from his new son-in-law. Before the arrival of his grandchildren, he was a strict army man with high standards, but a hidden soft heart. He was a brother to six siblings, four of whom are still alive; he considers them his best friends, as family remains his highest value. After the arrival of his lovely grandchildren, Nico's heart melted like a marshmallow, and all the hidden tenderness started pouring out on them. Alta remains the cornerstone of this big happy family, and their source of inspiration and love.

Nico & Alta happily married for 49 years!

The Angel of Mercy and Her Sunshine

"Love doesn't make the world go round...
Love is what makes the ride worthwhile."

— Franklin P. Jones

When life takes unexpected turns, people tend to be shocked and paralyzed. In the best cases they start wondering "how can they overcome the situation?" But what if this unexpected turn is the door to your lasting love? Interesting, isn't it?

Dessy Devassy was a 17-years-old girl studying nursing, when this happened to her. After completing her first year in college, she joined a hospital for in-house training. Dessy was there when Sirraj had a severe car accident and was admitted to the hospital. She did not get a chance to meet him in person at first. She only heard about him from friends and colleagues at the hospital and in the hostel where they were staying. After hearing about how decent this patient was, with a very gentle character, she felt curious to meet him and went for a visit. However, Sirraj was so arrogant with her that she decided not to see him again.

The next day, her professor assigned her this exact patient to write the notes about! She was a bit shy to go to his room after getting embarrassed on the first visit and had to take along a friend for support. Dessy thought she must be nice to him since he was her patient. He started becoming nicer to her in return. As part of her job, Dessy asked Sirraj about his family, health, and psychological condition. When the time came to present the case to her professor, she was presenting her recording about Sirraj, when he put music on and started dancing with one hand, since he could not move the rest of his body.

The professor did not mind such behaviour from a patient, but Dessy could not help laughing. From the professor's perspective that was not the best thing a nurse can do as a reaction to a patient's behaviour, so he got really angry, started shouting at her and threw her papers down in front of the patient. After leaving the room he gave Dessy additional writing and informed her that he was lowering her grade. Dessy went to her room and started crying. Her friend went to Sirraj and told him that because of his behaviour Dessy was being punished. Sirraj started thinking about what he did and called Dessy to his room.

When she went to the room, he saw that she was crying, and he apologized to her. She pretended not to mind what happened, but he told her that he knew everything from her friend. The next day Sirraj asked his friend to buy some chocolate and called Dessy again to his room, to give it to her and apologize again for what happened. She accepted the apology but refused the gift as she was not supposed to take anything from her patients. When he asked her to take one piece of chocolate only, she took it as a courtesy and left the room.

Holidays began and the in-house training in the hospital ended. Dessy distributed cakes to all her patients, including

Sirraj, and went back to college. Sirraj got Dessy's number from a common friend and started texting her. He wrote this in his first message: "Hi I am Sirraj and I am in love with you. I don't want to hide any feelings". For him it had been love at first sight. When he was arrogant with her during her first visit, he was not in a good mood due the fractures in his body and he did not want her to see him in that helpless situation.

From Dessy's side there was no initial spark of love or strong chemistry towards Sirraj. She did not want to have any committed relationship with him, because they were from different religions, as he is a Muslim, and she is a Cristian. She was afraid to be asked to change her religion. Dessy suggested that they can only be a patient and a nurse. Sirraj respected her wish and told her they would be only friends. They started texting from time to time.

Dessy had lost her father two years before meeting Sirraj and was missing him a lot. Sirraj was very supportive. She could share with him what she could not share with her mother, as she needed the kind of male support that Sirraj provided. He would listen to her openly and she felt safe to share with him everything and listen to his advice. Initially Dessy had no dreams about the relationship. All she wanted was to have a good job to support herself and her mom financially. With time she became so grateful for Sirraj's support and help. Three months later she started falling in love with him. Only then they had their first telephone call. By that time his condition had improved, and they started talking more often over the phone.

One year later they met each other again for the first time since the hospital. She saw a tall, large man standing in front of her, very different from the one she remembered. Having a petite body herself, she felt scared and shy. When she shared her feelings, he started laughing. He had gained a lot of weight while recovering in bed. After that day they kept meeting. His home was close to her college and he used to go to the college to see her. Their feelings developed with time, and after two years she finished her studies and moved to another place in India for work.

One year passed and they met again at a train station. He was still huge to her, but when she saw him, she had a spark in her eyes and realized that she was truly in love with him. Sirraj got a job in Dubai and moved away. Dessy's family started looking for proposals for her, and Sirraj called the mom to propose and informed her that he was in love with her daughter. Dessy's mother refused, because there were no Muslims in her community and she only knew about them from distorted social media, so she told Sirraj "You are not good... and you people get married to seven ladies at the same time. I am not going to accept your request".

Sirraj was in shock! He called Dessy and said "Your mom is crazy! Why does she tell me this?! I did not even ask you to change your religion!". Dessy called her mother and argued with her, but her mom insisted on refusing and started seeing other guys for her daughter. Dessy informed her mother that she would not marry anyone other than Sirraj. Two years later Dessy got a job offer from a clinic in Dubai, and after passing her exam, she moved there.

Sirraj was working in Jebel Ali. The second day after Dessy's arrival to Dubai he quit his job and got a new one closer to Dessy. One year later, Dessy went back home and started telling her relatives and the people in the community that she was in love with someone and wanted to marry him. Because he was from a different religion, they did not accept what she said and sent her to a retreat for a week, thinking that she had lost her mind. When it was over, she returned to Dubai.

Once she arrived, she called her mom to tell her that nothing had changed, and she still wanted to marry Sirraj. It was her first win! She convinced her mother and brother about her heart's desire. After that glory, Dessy and Sirraj decided to go back to India in May 2020 to have the wedding there, but a new obstacle arose. This time it was from nature; COVID-19 hit the whole world and India went into lockdown for a long time.

They decided to wait for the borders to open to travel back to India for the celebration. Several months later, on Tuesday 9th Feb 2021, Dessy texted me out of the blue to say "Hi dear, how are you? finally we are getting married on the coming Sunday 14th Feb 2021. I am in India now, and both families mine and his are okay with the marriage". It was wonderful news! I felt so happy for her. I believed that true love wins, and after 10 years of patience and resilience it finally did for them!

Dessy is now dreaming about their future life with their families and living happily as a loving husband and wife. They are now planning to migrate to Canada, and they have started some courses in preparation. Dessy describes this robust loving relationship as the sun and earth. If there is no sun it will be dark everywhere on earth, and, to her, if Sirraj is not there her life will be dark.

Dessy & Sirraj on their wedding day!

CHAPTER 6

Building a Happy Family

Families are the building blocks of societies.
When couples decide to raise their seed of love with
more love, understanding, compassion, acceptance,
and ultimate wisdom, we together can build a happier
society that leads to a happier world.

"Adolescents are not monsters. They are just people trying
to learn how to make it among the adults in the world,
who are probably not so sure themselves."

— VIRGINIA SATIR

A rguments between parents and their children will always be there until we start tackling them with love and wisdom. To do this we need to revisit our beliefs, to see how they were formed and if they are still serving us and our families. This requires more openness to new possibilities, among them the possibility that our kids will make choices different from ours. We need to give them freedom, while watching these seeds growing in their own way with curiosity, nourishing them with understanding and love.

In this chapter and the upcoming one you will be introduced to the following terms. They may have different meanings in other contexts, so I want to clarify their meanings here to avoid confusion:

★ **A system:** represents a group of people (two or more) connected together with some sort of relationship (ex: a couple, a couple and their children, a couple with their children and extended family, a team, …etc.).

★ **Roles:** a function that a person plays within a system. It could be emotional or physical.

★ **Constellation:** a therapeutic approach designed to help reveal the hidden dynamics in a family or relationship, in order to address any stressors impacting these relationships and heal them. It can also be used to gather a group of people around a topic to find solutions.

This chapter is very dear to my heart, as building happy families is the core of my business and I consider it the mission of my life. But to get here we had to go through all the previous stages. Now we are in a position where the family system starts forming. It is not the couple alone anymore. There are kids, grandparents, in-laws, and other relatives and friends.

As promised in my previous chapter, the remaining topics from my survey about challenges facing couples in the first three years of marriage will be discussed here. They include change, lack of awareness of roles and responsibilities, expectations and the shock that follows when expectations and reality don't match, interference by in-laws, financial issues, and life shifts. I want to remind you that these topics were not of my choice, they were the top answers of women and men from different ages and cultures about challenges facing couples.

I was privileged to work with one family system that most people would have considered ideal. I was surprised to discover the amount of loneliness and low self-worth the little girl was feeling, which was manifesting in seeking perfection and expressing anger whenever she made a mistake, or even when her mom made a mistake while helping her with school projects.

I closed our session with the exercise of "love loop" and recommended that the little girl needed to do the "I love myself game" exercise for several weeks before she was ready to express love towards any of her family members. The session was heavy for the little girl, and I had to end it early. I am sure that if I had dug deeper, I would have found that the root of the issue was something so simple that it would have been hard for any regular person to notice. This happens because we cannot control how human minds process the information they receive. It is difficult to predict the effect it will leave on their psyche throughout the years.

What happened during the session confirmed my belief about the necessity of coaching couples before they get married. It is as important as planning for their wedding day, but sadly not many people seem to realize this. I understand it is not an easy process. Facing the psyche, opening the doors of intangible feelings, and having to face the strong wave of emotions and uncertainties accompanying unexpected self-discoveries is not easy. They may fear going through painful layers at a time when they are only supposed to have happy experiences.

But coaching provides a safe container for all tough experiences, allowing them to surface and be accepted without judgment, protecting people's image of themselves and others. It is also crucial to seek guidance when new members (i.e., kids and in-laws) enter the couple system, as the relationships become more complex.

Forming the family system

In a nutshell, marriage is change. It is entering a new life and environment. It comes with the highest number of expectations we face at any time in life. When these expectations are unmet, couples are shocked and start feeling helpless. These expectations come from commercialized images about marriage or from the things we learned from parents and married siblings and friends. We unconsciously build a belief that this is how it is and how it should be for us. The problem is, no matter how familiar we are with our original families and their systems, we are still different human beings who come with new tastes, thoughts, desires, behaviours, and preferences.

When we expect our spouse to conform with our system and start putting him/her within this container, deciding for them how they should or shouldn't be, we are limiting the relationship and not giving it the space to grow. Each starts pulling the other in their direction, thinking that this is the right thing to do. Conformity brings a lot of fights along the way. Things get even worse when extended family and friends start giving opinions about how the couple should or shouldn't live their lives. Couples often make the mistake of letting others have a say in their relationship and lives.

I have heard interesting stories about in-laws who wanted their sons to marry girls based on their taste. They only cared to choose someone who was like them, fitting in their container, without caring if she connected well to their son or not. There are also parents who want the man to be exactly like them, not caring about their daughter's preferences. This creates a lot of voids in the new marriage; people feel confined and lacking the freedom to be who they are or bring their uniqueness to it. This extends to children and grandchildren, as every generation complies with the older one. We end up having torn systems with weak relationships in total confusion.

Oftentimes, people use superficial ways to strengthen their connection, like visiting each other more, spending longer hours in the same place, or texting and talking a lot, while their souls are disconnected. This results in more separation, loneliness, dissatisfaction and less joy. The solution is to regain our freedom to choose and be, to live our lives on our own terms, even if they are different from those of our parents and grandparents, and to raise our children to have the same freedom. This will allow us to bring our uniqueness to the new family system (consisting of the couple and their kids) and strengthen our relationships with love.

Only then we can bring more love to our extended family and friends. If our new-born system is weak, it becomes a burden and we become dependent on our parents, relatives and friends to solve our problems. They will never be able to do it, as we are the only experts of our own lives. Likewise, our spouses don't need to have a say on how our original families live. We need to establish healthy boundaries, starting with the self, so that neither the original family nor the spouse invades the personal territory of the other.

Planting the seed

When conception happens and the baby starts growing inside the mother's womb, they become like one unit together, feeding on the same food, sharing the same water intake, moving, sleeping and doing everything together. The baby is totally dependent on the mother's body for life. When the baby is born, a physical separation happens that requires grief. Because taking the baby out of his/her mother's womb is a kind of loss. Oftentimes mothers fail to grieve this loss and keep thinking about babies as a continuation of them.

It is fair to say that fathers think the same way, but it is more obvious with mothers, due to the physical connection. Another aspect related to the birth process is the introduction of a new element to the system, which used to consist of the couple alone or them and their in-laws. And now comes the baby too. It is a process that throws the system into chaos. How are they going to deal with this little human being? It takes time until they figure out their way, while practicing different new behaviours, until the new element (the baby) becomes a natural part of the system and the new status quo is formed.

For babies it is a different story. They want to figure out the world around them. They need to form a view about themselves and others and learn how others view them. It is a whole new world, one where they gradually develop an interdependent self. Babies use three ways to communicate their needs and desires:

★ **Crying for almost everything:** To eat, to have their diaper changed, when they feel in pain, scared or lonely...etc.

★ **Skin colour:** this conveys important information about their health. They also learn new information through touching and sensing the vibration of adults' voices through their skin. When adults say loving words but hold the baby firmly, out of fear, this fearful feeling is transferred to the baby through the skin and becomes associated in their memory with the event. If anyone later holds them in the same way, even if they say loving words, the grownup kids will feel scared.

★ **Breathing:** Babies communicate their feelings through their breathing. It requires good observation to understand their breathing patterns.

The way adults respond to babies' actions plays a vital role in building their psyche and self-image. It tells them whether it is okay to express themselves and how their needs will be met when voiced. It is important to talk to the baby and always explain that any reaction we take has nothing to do with their identity, and that we love them no matter what. If we don't do this, babies and kids will take our initial messages of anger, fear or any unhappy emotion as a trusted truth without negotiation. They will believe that they are unworthy. Babies need their parents to show them how to survive physically and psychologically without damaging their self-image.

To encourage their growth, we need to let them practise their five freedoms: the freedom to hear and see what is going on, rather than being told they are too young for it; the freedom to feel their feelings and express them without judgment, whether it is a boy who wants to cry or a girl who is feeling angry and wants to show her anger; the freedom to think in their own way and share their thoughts with us even if they are different from what we think; the freedom to ask for what they want instead of always waiting for our permission; and the freedom to risk trying new things on their own behalf, rather than having their life experiences limited by over-protection.

Once they develop this holistic freedom at home and grow with high self-worth, believing that their parents will love them no matter what, they can start connecting with people from a healthy and loving place. They will be able to form healthy relationships with their friends and classmates, act kindly to the older generation and extended family members, and offer help to humans in need. This is because their emotional tank is full already, and they are ready to become great contributors to the world, spreading happiness, peace and love everywhere they go.

Roles and responsibilities

From my personal experience and observation, in addition to the survey's answers, I have noticed that at least 50% of conflicts in families and relationships arise from a lack of clarity, misunderstanding, and disagreement about roles and responsibilities. These roles are:

★ **Conscious/outer roles** in the physical realm like cooking, cleaning, dropping kids to school or helping them to study, earning money and spending it.

★ **Unconscious/inner emotional roles** that are needed to serve the relationship, like the decision-maker, nurturer, leader, listener, empath...etc. These roles can come in opposites where one of them complements the other. This explains why narcissists (excessive takers) blend very well with co-dependents (excessive givers) for the relationship to reach a balance point.

A lot of misconception is built around roles due to social conditioning. Some roles are so associated with certain family members that a trial of switching them can become a catastrophic event. Let's say there is a family consisting of a working father, a housewife and three children. There is an agreement (conscious or unconscious) that the mother helps kids in their studies. If the family goes through a financial crisis, the mom might start working to earn money and support her family. Her time becomes as limited as the father's. Rather than being flexible and sharing the role of helping kids in their studies, the father allows resistance to arise, leading to conflict.

Parents may start using toxic behaviours like blaming or being defensive as a coping mechanism. It puts the family in more trouble than they initially had, especially when these behaviours filter down to kids. They may blame themselves for what happened, affecting their self-worth and their behaviour to the outer world. It may also lead to agitation and physical illness. What would help, is to consider what is happening as uncontrollable change, which normally comes with chaos and frustration. With more collaboration and love it can be resolved.

Family dynamics

Some roles exist because the system needs them to create balance. For example, if someone in the family is a troublemaker and travels abroad, another person will pick his/her role and keep playing it until the system stops needing it. When parents complain about their children's behaviour, whether a kid or a teenager, it usually turns out that the child is voicing a suppressed need in the system through their behaviour. For example: voicing the need of a father to spend more time with his kids, the mom to listen to them more, or the need for more freedom of choice.

These voices or needs are usually suppressed for a long time; that's why their manifestation, when it comes, is intense and shocking. Suppressed voices will only get louder until we attend to the original need. This explains the tendency of some family members to become addicted to food, drugs, shopping, playing games, or going out a lot and avoiding being at home. They want to numb these intense voices as they don't know how to express them in healthy ways, especially when the family is not opened to influence or suggestion.

Emotions or voices rotate in the family system, exactly as water transfers between connected compartments of a water tank. When a compartment undergoes high pressure, water in that compartment moves to one with lower pressure. Emotions do the same, when a family member suppresses his/her feelings, they find their way to the next unresisting member to be voiced. I have included in the exercises section a constellation to help you deal with suppressed voices and learn about your family system's needs.

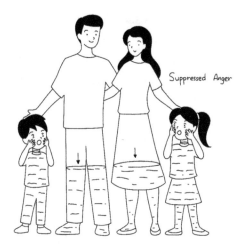

Suppressed Anger

Financial battles

"We create a happier world by fairly distributed responsibilities and rewards, which can only be achieved through collaboration."

— REEM AHMED

Money management and the quality of relationships between couples and family members are strongly interrelated. In my survey, arguments around money and financial issues appeared in almost 80% of the answers. When money management is poor, conflicts arise. Likewise, when people have low-quality relationships, their financial management strategies are affected, leading to conflicts and dissatisfaction about all material things. The way couples communicate and cope with financial stresses significantly impacts the quality of their relationships.

Financial battles start when people have different values, unconscious beliefs and perceptions. One partner perceiving the other partner as a spendthrift can cause conflicts. What one person considers a need, the other might see as a luxury. For example, spending money on healthy food and exercising will be a need for someone who values living a healthy lifestyle, whereas it can appear as unnecessary spending for a person who does not. A husband who loves travelling, learning and technology, can face difficulty justifying spending money on these things if his wife does not see their value.

Such beliefs cause members of the family to build expectations on how everyone should or shouldn't think, feel and behave with money. The tricky part is that these beliefs are built on the subconscious level. The person himself/herself may not be aware of them and cannot clearly articulate them to others. This can be handled with flexibility and openness to see the other person's view of the world with a curious mindset.

When a husband has a tight income, with financial worries and insecurities, and does not talk about money, his wife may unconsciously play the role of a "financial manager" to participate in money matters. Clear communication about financial roles and responsibilities, management practices, needs and desires can prevent many financial problems from happening. Changing behaviours and perceptions about money and spending can improve and strengthen the relationship, even when conflicts have already taken place.

Life shifts and turning points

*"Life is what happens to you while you are busy
making other plans."*

— JOHN LENNON

When we face obstacles in life, like financial difficulties, illness or accidents, we can either resist them and keep questioning why such things are happening to us, or we can choose to surrender to whatever is happening, believing that it is happening for a good reason. This requires faith and management of expectations from ourselves and others, understanding that we are all humans who may at times make wrong choices. They could be choosing the wrong behaviour in a situation, having thoughts that don't serve us, or taking actions that don't bring the results we want. The good news is that these mistakes provide us with valuable information to choose better next time.

Once we surrender, we allow ourselves to ponder how we can bring more love to ourselves, our spouses and children, and the people around us, to navigate through the situation peacefully.

It is really important to be inclusive in our thinking about solutions. We cannot think of loving ourselves and blaming our spouse, children or even life events. At the same time, we cannot be loving to others and ignore ourselves. It is crucial to include everyone involved, as the effect of the disaster is cumulative, even if we cannot see it, and its solution has to bring happiness to all too. When we do this the answers appear before our eyes in easy and unexpected ways.

Exercise 6.1: *Love loop*

Love loop is an extended version of the "love conversations" exercise in the previous chapter. It helps enhance relationships within your family. It shifts the emotional field (atmosphere) between family members, from jealousy and criticism to finding something to value about the other person.

1. Sit in a circle with all family members.
2. Decide who will start and how you want to rotate between members. Make sure that everyone is included in the exercise.
3. Start by saying "I love you, (name of the first member), I really do".
4. "I love in you…" and mention their personal, physical, emotional, and intellectual traits. Say whatever you love about them, search, dig deeper, I am sure you'll find something, resting assured that you'll get love in return.
5. Let them say "I know, thank you! and I love in you…", mentioning all the personal, physical, emotional and intellectual traits they appreciate.
6. Then you will also say "I know, thank you!".
7. Rotate between members, ensuring that everyone in the loop expresses love to everyone else. People in a group may have a tendency to express love to certain members and not to others. Be careful, this creates an unhealthy atmosphere. Everyone must feel loved and accepted by everyone else for healthier and happier relationships.
8. Repeat the exercise every week.

Exercise 6.2: Hearing suppressed voices

As mentioned earlier, sometimes your family system has needs (i.e., freedom, care, love…etc.) that have been suppressed for a long time. The emotion associated with the need (i.e., anger, sadness, jealousy…etc.) keeps rotating between family members until it gets voiced by the least resistant one, who is ready to express it through his/her behaviours. Do the following exercise with the conscious intention of listening to the system's needs. Be ready to receive the message, accept it and learn the lesson it is carrying with love:

1. Write the different inner roles (i.e., decision-maker, nurturer, leader, listener, empath…etc.) and outer roles (i.e., mother, father, daughter, worker, cooker, cleaner…etc.)

of your system on pieces of papers and put them randomly on the ground.

2. Make sure to add some blank papers for any new role that may be required or that you were not unaware of before.
3. Allow different family members to occupy these roles by standing on the papers.
4. Let them choose where they want to stand and start talking about the role, its responsibilities and needs.
5. Listen to what every member has to say and allow other members to reply to him/her.
6. Avoid judgment, criticism or blame. Just allow the wisdom of the system to come out through your family members' voices.
7. Based on the learned information, think about inclusive solutions in which everyone is contributing and feeling loved and appreciated.
8. Create a plan for how you want to implement these solutions within your family. Ensure to have consensus, where everyone promises to collaborate in the solution and to keep their promise.
9. Decide on how you will know these solutions are in place. Are you going to observe each other and give kind and loving feedback? Do you prefer written reminders? Is each member going to jot down their progress in their daily journal and inform the rest about it when s/he feels convenient?
10. Start with the easiest step possible and move to the harder ones gradually, to build easy momentum and avoid resistance, which may arise if the shift from one status to another is taken in one sharp leap.

11. Have fun while doing it to lighten the atmosphere. Be mindful of sensitive members.
12. Agree on the next time you want to listen to the system's wisdom, to ensure it is an ongoing process.

If you come with a closed mindset that resists influence, none of what I mentioned in this chapter will work for you or your family. In order to build a happy and healthy family you need to be willing to try new beliefs, behaviours, roles and responsibilities. You need to operate from a place of collective love for the whole system all the time, neither ignoring your needs to satisfy others nor overlooking the needs of others to fulfil yours.

You also need to learn how to be independent of your extended family members when it comes to the way you are raising your kids and running your life with your spouse. Firmly place loving, healthy boundaries between your extended family and your immediate family, so that no one invades the territory of the other. It is important that all members treat each other with tremendous respect and acceptance. And if you have any issues with the word freedom, maybe it is time to build a new concept about it and embrace it. It will bring the best out of you and every member of the family.

Before allowing your extended family to shape your family through their beliefs and opinions, stop and think "Does this work for the best of all? How will this make my spouse or children feel? Will they feel safe? Will they see me as a highly unpredictable person, being affected by different opinions? Think how such unpredictability can jeopardize the health and happiness of the newly born family.

You also need to develop the right garden for your kids to flourish and develop into the amazing human beings they are meant to be. Teach them how to love and be loved and build happy and healthy relationships with them, based on acceptance and understanding of differences. Make your decisions for them from a loving place, based on what will make them happy in the long run, not based on your own perspectives. Don't assume that they must be like you no matter what. Encourage their mental and spiritual growth, in addition to their physical growth, by letting them practise their five freedoms.

It is also important to understand the roles and responsibilities in your system and treat them with flexibility, allowing all members to play different roles at different times. When a voice in your system calls for your attention, listen to it with curiosity and love, use the message to grow and deepen your family bonds. When life shifts hit your system, refrain from blaming and look for a way to bring a collaborative solution that will be good for all.

Make sure your kids will grow to have high self-esteem, believing that they are loved no matter what, even when they make wrong choices in life. This will fill their emotional tank and they will be able to connect to extended family, colleagues, friends and people in the world with love and kindness. And they will be able to spread the message of love and peace to the whole world.

Unify your efforts as a family to shift the focus from individuals to the relationships between them and the family dynamics. Make sure to understand and teach your children the importance of roles and responsibilities. Keep rotating them to avoid any role saturation, which may lead to resistance or depression. Understand that our lives are not predictable no matter how well we plan them. There will always be life shits and turning points that we need to surrender to, to be able to think clearly and find inclusive solutions for all family members.

After working so hard on yourself to become the best loving human you can and to become connected lovingly with your friends, spouse and family members to form a healthy family that vibrates peace and happiness, you can increase the ripple to the whole world. In the next chapter we will learn how kids raised with love (i.e., our new ambassadors) can create a happier world by spreading the message of love.

The Opposite Turning into the Soulmate

"Who knows what is good and what is bad?"

— ANONYMOUS

*H*ere is a story of a loving and intriguing relationship between two soulmates who never expected to be so. Its heroine is my dear friend and genius physiotherapist, Shaimy Ittoop. When I asked Shaimy if she had a positive and successful loving relationship that she wanted to speak about to inspire the world, she replied without hesitation, "Absolutely, my relationship with my dear husband Sivachand! It is a loving marriage. It has been four years since we got married, and I consider it a very positive relationship".

Shaimy's story did not start with a love spark of any kind. It rather started with consistent grind and irritation! Shaimy's husband was her classmate in college. He was the opposite of the kind of person she would normally be attracted to. For example, he prefers to deal with life as it comes, and she loves to have everything planned and in order. At the beginning, her prevailing feeling was total irritation with him.

But he was smart and took it lightly. He didn't do things to please her or try to be different so that she would like him. Instead, he turned the irritating aspects of his character into positive qualities in her eyes. Whenever she felt annoyed by him, he would do or say something to make her laugh. Rather than linking his behaviour to something negative in her mind, she started accepting his difference. With time she started noticing other positive qualities in him.

Shaimy had many colleagues at college. All of them would do things to get something in return, except Sivachand. He would always give without expecting something in return. He gave just for the sake of giving, not for the sake of getting. This ignited the spark of attraction and love in her heart. Shaimy found him kind and interesting! This trait of selflessness was enough to bring her closer to him and grow love in her heart, until they decided to get married.

When they started planning for their wedding ceremony, Shaimy experienced the hardest moment in the relationship. They came from different religions. There are many differences in the cultures and their rituals. Her society, as she described, has many restrictions and obligations, which she always wanted to leave behind.

After long discussions, they decided to follow her religion and culture in the ceremony, and then each of them would keep his/her religion and practise their own rituals. Shaimy attended a lot of classes to get prepared for this big change, some on her own and others with her parents. She learned how to get accustomed to this new life, while at the same time keeping her own faith and religion.

During those four years of marriage Shaimy and her husband have faced a lot of challenges. She had to come to Dubai alone, at a time when they were dreaming of having a baby. The husband followed her to Dubai, but it took him a while to settle and find a job. They overcame all of those challenging times together, with grace and peace, especially because her husband is a very positive, easy-going person, and does not take things seriously.

Although Shaimy used to be a very serious and punctual person, she has learned from him to deal with life lightly. They don't plan for the future and live life as it comes. This shift was not easy for Shaimy, but she realized that when she plans and has high expectations, she feels sad or disappointed if those expectations are not met. So, she decided to plan less and live in the moment, exactly like her husband.

Shaimy is living her dream now. She does not think of any other dreams or aspirations. But she knows her husband's strong passion for football, and that he is fantasizing about going to the Emirates Football Stadium in London; her love to him made her adopt his dream and decide to make it hers too. Shaimy feels he is not only her husband, but also her close friend to whom she can tell anything and everything.

Shaimy and Sivachand celebrating their child's birthday

Living in Balance – Self Actualization & Happy Family

*"Family is the link to the past,
and the bridge to the future."*

— ANONYMOUS

*E*ven arranged marriages succeed when they are nurtured with respect and understanding. It all depends on your goals, preferences and model of the world. Noha's dream was to have a successful career and build a happy family with a kind and honest husband, who would express his feelings openly, speak his mind frankly, and communicate with her directly.

At the early stages of her life, she only focused on studying and having a good job. She was not thinking about marriage at all. After completing her master's degree and finding a very good job, she thought that she had accomplished her career goal, and it was time for her to settle down and have a family. At that stage she was mature enough to make this move. She appreciates the family atmosphere and loves kids.

Romance was not a target for her at all. She wasn't looking for someone to fall in love with, but someone to form a family with. She was thinking about it with her mind, and not with her heart. Noha was referred to Adanan through family friends, and they arranged a formal family date. There was no spark of attraction until she started talking to him. She asked him a few questions and he answered her truthfully. It clicked with what she was looking for. She used to be very sceptical and had refused many proposals because the proposed men were not honest with her; this time she had a sense of acceptance and relief.

When the potential father-in-law saw her, he liked her on the spot. He had a strong personality. Because Adnan had refused many girls before Noha, his father wanted to finish everything fast. The marriage was arranged quickly. Noha now loves her husband and has a very happy family with four kids. She feels a nice balance and synchronicity between her mind and heart. She is fantasizing about sustaining the intimacy in her marriage and the understanding between herself and her husband.

Noha wants him to continue being the supportive person he is for her career growth and ambitions. She does not like to be controlled or forced to accept the options of others. And her husband was so understanding and supportive of her needs at the beginning. She aspires for this support to remain and grow even more.

Any human being who loves something sometimes experiences fear of losing it. Noha is having those fears. She fears that her husband might change, and they might start having unresolved conflicts or differences in opinions that they cannot embrace. She is also afraid that her in-laws might start interfering in her life. She is an independent person, one who does not like to be dissolved in her husband or make her life centred around him. Even if (GOD forbid) such conflicts happen, causing them to travel into two different paths, she will still live her life with grace and happiness.

Noha believes that any relationship can go through tough times. We can look at it as a scale managed by two parties. When one of them goes down the other can balance it with more understanding and support. In such a way, tough times will pass away easily. My wish for this amazing soul and very mature mind is to continue her happy and healthy relationship with her partner until she witnesses her grandchildren. I hope that she experiences not only the same level of success, depth and happiness in her relationship, but also everything she aspires to in life. More success, warmth, depth, understanding, love, and happiness in all directions, shapes and forms.

SECTION 5

Towards a Happier World

CHAPTER 7

Creating a Happier World

We all dream of a peaceful and joyful world. Creating this world cannot be achieved without loving, tranquil, compassionate individuals, ready to build heathy families, more cohesive societies and a happier world.

"There is no path to peace, peace is the path."

— MAHATMA GANDHI

How many sad stories do you hear every day compared to the happy ones? How many people do you see laughing deeply from the heart? How many friends share their joyful moments without hesitation? How many acquaintances are not complaining? It is evident how distressed the world has become. TV shows, sad songs, bullying at school and work, friends and relatives arguing all the time, married couples fighting, colleagues betraying each other, managers abusing their team members emotionally, mentally, and intellectually, wars and bombs, killing, addiction…etc. People have become so attuned to misery to the point that commercials use it to attract more audience.

Think about the times when you wanted something badly, waited for it so long, and when it happened you started thinking "I can't believe it! I am afraid something will go wrong!" As if happiness cannot happen without a sad event following it! In this chapter I am calling you to change your perception by action. A happier world is like a relationship; it cannot happen by itself; we rather create it and keep replenishing it all the time.

This book is structured to build a global system one brick at a time. At this point, I am discussing an intricate kind of connection, comprising composite differences not only between individuals, but also between the systems they represent. By the end of this chapter, you will understand how our global misery can be eliminated, utilizing the power of love. I mean fairly distributed unconditional love for every human being on earth, regardless of who they are, what they own or what title they hold. The responsibility of distributing it is also given to all humans to implement at the level of their lives, in order for this worldly mission to be accomplished on a mega level.

How many of you can remember being bullied at school, at a social gathering or a workplace? Let me share with you a personal story that happened several years ago. I am a very quiet person who has spent my whole life with books and not socializing much. I had a family consisting of eight older siblings and tight finances. I used to spend summer holidays at home reading biographies, cycling in the yard or going to the public library.

I had a belief that people always mean what they say, or at least express what they think and feel honestly. When I joined the workforce, I was a fresh graduate holding my BSc in Computer Science, without much experience about people's behaviour. My formula for success was do your work, mind your own business and go home, just like college: study hard, comprehend, do well in exams and you get the 'A'. But it was not that simple.

This incident happened soon after I was hired. I was standing alone outside our department next to the handrail on the second floor when a colleague I did not have any conflict with before, walked up to me and said "Reem, how about me throwing you down from here?" Feeling shocked I simply replied, "You can throw yourself if you want, why throw me?". She said "Well, no, I have a husband and a daughter who want me, you don't have anyone who wants you"! What ridiculous reasoning for such an unhealthy behaviour!

I was speechless. I went home upset and told my mother what happened, and her comment was "Girls get jealous; don't bother about it". I felt confused! Why would such a pretty girl feel jealous of me?! She had a great job as an IT engineer, doing more interesting tasks than I was allowed to do. She was at a higher grade with a higher salary, was married to a man she said loved her, and had a beautiful daughter. Why would someone like that feel jealous of me?!

At that time, I measured things with a paper and a pen. Now I realize that there are things much deeper in the human psyche, things that cannot be seen but only sensed. My awareness has improved with years of reading, observing, studying, failing, crying, reflecting and trying again, so I can now see what was happening with more awareness and understanding.

When I was minding my own business, working hard and going home, this woman thought I was arrogant. Her outer possession gave her the false impression that her higher rank meant that I must approach her to try to win her over to become my friend. When I did not do that, she decided to attack my core of self-worth to bring me down. The best way she found was to remind me that I don't have a husband and a daughter. Unfortunately, due to my level of awareness at that time, she succeeded.

One of the biggest mistakes we make is measuring people's worth based on how many things on the checklist of outer belongings they possess. Their position, gender, age, nationality, how much money they have…etc. You might think this way of thinking is out of date. Let me whisper the truth: "It is not! It is becoming modernized, commercialized, beautified with nice false words, but it is not eliminated".

How many of us have had to endure such social poison, where our self-worth was on the edge? All of us want to belong. Being rejected or called to obey and conform, which is a form of rejection, is exactly like saying "You are not loved! You have no value! You cannot exist in this world!". Every human being wants to know they are okay and not rejected for the same exact reason. That reason is love.

Living in a traumatized world

The world is so accustomed to living in sadness and pain. I had one of the worst experiences in my last job. I tried every solution possible, but my managers stood firm on their toxic behaviours, without a willingness to change. At that time, I was posting about a variety of things on social media. Some posts were about lessons learned, awareness gained and wisdom. Other posts expressed my sad experience. I noticed that the number of responses to my posts about extreme vulnerability was much higher than for those on lessons learned, which was good and bad at the same time.

It was good to show compassion to someone in pain, but bad if people can only connect with the pain and don't care about the gained wisdom. What intrigued me most were the people who called on me to suppress my feelings, either directly by saying don't cry or don't complain, or indirectly by stopping their communication when I spoke the truth. When people call for conformity without realizing it, they show a kind of social programming, causing many others to suppress their feelings when they try to connect, seek solutions or gain empathy. By doing this they are hiding important information from surfacing – about deep needs to be fulfilled, actions to be taken, and things to be given attention.

When people are exposed to resentful actions long enough, the cumulative effect throws them into trauma, deep wounds, and suffering. They make one of two choices, either activating their inner wolves or their inner heroes, causing their psyche to develop either into someone who wants misery for everyone else, or someone who wants to protect others from living similar experiences. The longer someone travels in one direction, the more familiar and easier it becomes.

People who choose to activate their inner wolves, start performing one unloving action after the other. They sink deeper into guilt, shame, and self-hatred, causing them to want to drag others into their swamp. This reminds me of the monkey paradigm. Scientists put a group of monkeys in a big cage with bananas hanging from the top of the cage. Whenever a monkey jumped to get one, the scientists would hit him with a stick. After many unsuccessful trials, the monkeys stopped trying. A new monkey got introduced to the cage, when he naturally jumped to pick a banana, the older monkeys hit him to get down.

I see the majority of people operating from fear, competition and a desire to prove themselves. Everyone wants to know they are okay and ensure that their self-esteem is not injured. They tip-toe around each other, thinking "Oh! What if they use this information to shame or manipulate me one day? What will happen to my self-worth?!" or "Oh! What if they grow and start competing with me? What will happen to my value in society? How will I be able to exist on earth?" or "Oh! What if they think badly about me and stop loving me?".

People tend to protect themselves by hiding their weaknesses and shaming people who show them and tell their truth. They become dominant by not allowing others to grow, containing them in one way or another. They believe, falsely, that this will guarantee them love, protection from harm, self-worth, and societal value. Guess what? None of this will serve them in the long run. It is a fragile shell that may work once or even 100 times, but there will be a time when it does not, and when this happens their pain will be extravagant. When people operate consistently from fear, they tend to do things they will not be happy about later.

Our world is living in collective trauma. Small hurts seem unimportant until they develop into deeper wounds. We see a co-dependent wife reaching the point where she can no longer forgive her narcissistic husband, using every chance possible to point out his mistakes in an exaggerated way. When he gets feds up with her behaviour, he starts shouting at her, throwing her into a victim mindset. The main issue is deep, unspoken wounds that have not received the attention required to heal. I wish we could eliminate these issues at an early stage before they escalate and develop.

People are blindly following social pre-conditioning. They say they don't agree with these social rules, without realizing that they deeply believe in them. It manifests through their words and actions whenever their beliefs are tested. Many people give themselves the permission to decide for others what suits them according to the pre-conditioning they unconsciously follow without caring to ask others with pure empathy "what do they really want for themselves?". People are unconsciously stealing each other's freedom of choice, which is a human birthright. And when they experience the pain of not having this freedom for themselves it is intolerable.

Societies are numbed. Talking about emotions is shameful and unwelcome. Many companies steal their employee's freedom, not allowing them to have a balanced and healthy lifestyle, through rigidity, rules antagonistic to human nature, and carelessness about their emotions and needs. Managers make employees feel rejected, using their authority to refuse almost every single request that can help them regain balance.

People stab each other in the back while smiling to their faces. Friends appear helpful, but the dark side of their jealousy slips in through their words. Tortured souls want to see others suffering. Psychologically unstable people refuse to work on their wounds, giving free rein to their inner monsters to put others in pain.

We need to pay attention to the effect of those wounds before they escalate and become uncontrollable, when the number of addicted teenagers, divorced couples, stealing, violence, and physical abuse becomes intolerable, demanding an instant solution. Because solutions in those cases may work, but in many cases are not sustainable. Such unhealthy symptoms keep showing up through different people, dragging our attention to the need of love, belonging, and freedom of being. And the cycle continues until this need is satisfied. Mother Theresa once said, "The hunger for love is much more difficult to remove than hunger for bread".

Healing the collective trauma

What would help is digging deeper to understand the root causes of the problem. What were people's feelings about themselves when they decided to act in such ways? This must be done with a lot of care about the human psyche and without shaming or blaming them, without saying "How could you do this? You have low self-worth and self-love!". Again, I am not condoning the maladaptive behaviour, I am rather calling for infusing more love, understanding, acceptance, honesty, wisdom and kindness. We need to encourage congruency and compassion to one another, without limitations or discrimination. No one can be excused while the other is criminalized. No one ranks higher than others. And no one is seen as better than others.

Is this an easy process? No, but the results are worth the journey. Will it happen quickly? That depends on how much we are in consensus with those concepts. Some may keep working on their inner peace, but as crossing their edge will make others responsible to cross theirs too (which they may not want or be ready for) they will face a lot of resistance, get pulled backwards, as happened in the monkey paradigm. You may think it is scary! Yes, it is. It requires courage to initiate the process and call for change.

We need the right support system, one that embraces change and allows expression of all kinds of emotions, like worry and anger, as part of their human rights. What scares people about anger is the meaning they give it. Anger is habitually associated with physical violence, which is not fair. Anger by itself is not harmful. It is an important emotion informing us that something is out of balance. It requires appreciation, listening to its message with compassion, and using it to do things better.

While anger is a healthy emotion, suppressed anger is harmful. It fuels the emotions until they cross the threshold of tolerance and are expressed suddenly with full force. This is what causes violence to happen, a long-suppressed emotion bursts and gets expressed in a kind of overdose. Remember, any suppressed voice will only get louder. Whether it is anger or any other emotion. After giving room for anger, fear and worry to be expressed in a healthy way, we allow other emotions such as appreciation to surface. Then the new learning comes naturally.

These emotions are natural feelings when people experience something new or different. Like meeting a person from another culture or ethnicity, change in work processes, taking decisions for our lives that society is not familiar with, someone using different expressions than what we use, or people introducing different food. We need to develop tolerance to those emotions at early stages, respecting their existence, and all will be well.

When two systems collide

Conflicts create heat and escalate to wars when people don't have the capacity or willingness to endure their inevitable difference. It puts the whole system on fire, and everyone suffers the consequence. We see direct and indirect calls for conformity and obedience. People of higher rank, like managers and business owners, oscillate between active and passive-aggressive moods, without attending to how their actions affect the emotional field governing their relationships with others.

Members of such unhealthy systems are not allowed to voice their thoughts or possess their birthrights and needs as humans:

★   Their right to see and hear what is happening instead of what should be, was or will be.
★   Their right to feel their feelings freely.
★   Their right to express their thoughts and feelings.
★   Their right to ask for what they want instead of always waiting for permission.
★   Their right to take risks on their own behalf.

When the obedient person tries to reclaim their freedom to exercise their birthrights, they are pushed back and ordered to suppress them. I have seen this happening a lot in families, between friends and at workplace.

What people with higher ranks (i.e., managers, parents, the wealthy ...etc.) don't realize is that any system will always work towards equilibrium, creating roles filled by different members to voice its needs. Unaware of this, they tend to stop those below them from expressing themselves, through punishment or manipulation. It is important to satisfy the need of the system, by pondering why this role appeared in the first place. Even if a member exhausts his/her energy to deliver the message of wisdom, and leaves the system, another member either new or existing will take over the role, until the system's need for change is met.

When individuals acting as messengers of their system come in contact, acceptance of difference must occur on both sides. When human freedoms aren't respected or welcomed, they start resisting each other. Those with the least tolerance to diversity (in thoughts, beliefs, attitudes, physical appearance... etc.) will show rejection first. Anger develops in the emotional field. When people choose to react rather than be proactive, each heated emotion leads to the next. The system becomes highly charged, causing it and all its members to be on edge.

What would help instead is stepping back and taking a helicopter view without emotional attachment. From this neutral position, people can make a conscious decision to switch roles, to experience what is happening in the opposite system, embodying their conditions and experiencing their emotions. The result is more awareness and understanding about each other's experience, and the effect of their actions, now and in the future. Bear in mind that conflicts will still arise, as differences will always be there, but people can approach them differently and more consciously.

Building a healthier community

Building healthier, more loving and cohesive communities is a natural by-product of our work to this point. We have focused on human rebirth and building happier families one at a time; on how the children of those families become their loving ambassadors in the world, carrying the flag of love and working towards a more cohesive society. Their mission in any situation will always be "How can I bring more love to myself, you, and the whole world?".

They will infuse more understanding, tolerance, and acceptance in workplaces, beyond jealousy, aggressive competition, and thoughts about who is taking more than whom. They will base their actions on fairness, wanting for others what they want for themselves, no more and no less. Because all are equal in their worthiness of love. They will be able to establish healthy boundaries between their work and personal lives, so that neither leaks its stresses into the other nor takes their attention away from the important things in their lives. They will create a balance that brings them peace and happiness.

Believing in their self-worth, they will make their decisions based on desire, not need. They'll know that no matter where they go, they can put their strengths to use and contribute to success. They'll have the capacity to give and receive love freely and congruently, through kind words and action in every relationship they have, without pretending or hiding their feelings. They'll know that all their needs and feelings are valid, and they'll have the freedom to express them and ask for what they want in all areas of life.

When they operate from this place, people who also have high self-worth will accept their difference, allowing them to express their thoughts and needs freely, without pushing them away or shutting them off. They'll feel safe and assured that allowing others to be themselves does not threaten their existence or the amount of love they will receive. They will be full of love from the inside. There will be no place for jealousy or hurtful competition. It will only motivate them to show more kindness and love towards self and others, without wearing masks or needing anyone's approval of their actions. This is because they will know, deeply, that it is coming from a place of pure love.

Magnifying the ripple of love

When I think about our mission on earth, two things come to my mind: worshipping GOD out of love and gratitude rather than fear; and building earth, which is the legacy that we'll leave behind. I do believe the best state to leave earth, for the generations to come, is a state of happiness, coming from tremendous inner and outer peace and harmony between people and unconditional love.

This may sound like a big promise, but as a coach I have learned that any goal is achievable, once it is broken into smaller pieces and targets are set. When we apply this concept to building earth and having a happier world for people to live in, we can set smaller targets of building happier cohesive societies. As families are the building blocks of societies, we can start there. But in order to have a happy family, we need to have two happy people bonding with love, transferring this love and happiness to their children and grandchildren. So, to have a loving, happier, and more peaceful world, we need to develop happier, loving and more peaceful individuals first.

I understand that we can't ask an injured person to giggle out of joy before treating their wounds. We must heal any trauma first, regardless of its source – war, natural disaster, a dysfunctional family, or toxic partners or co-workers. The result is the same: an injured soul who needs to heal. Whether this trauma happened 10 years, six months, or two weeks ago, attention has to be called to it first.

When these wounds are healed, individuals need to be introduced to their true selves, to get to know themselves all over again, to connect to their thoughts and feelings and express them freely. They need to cultivate their self-image in a different way than when they overcame their previous hurdles. And connect with love to other human beings. We must keep this mission in front of our eyes all the time, keep navigating new zones of self, emotions, thoughts, and other people's differences with patience, diligence, acceptance and persistence, to build a happier world together.

Exercise 7.1: Discovering self-responsibility for a happier world

In this exercise we are going to constellate the world's systems around peace and love. It requires at least eight people. Seven of them will represent the world's continents and one will observe from outside.

1. Write on a piece of paper the words peace and love and place it on the ground in the middle of the group to represent our mission of achieving a loving peace and a peaceful love.

Not peace that comes at any price. And not love expressed in unkind ways.

2. Write the continents' names, followed by the word 'societies' on papers, toss them on the ground and leave them to settle where they land.
3. Write the words 'differences', 'conflicts', 'traumas', 'healing', 'families', 'individuals', 'passions', 'congruence', 'kindness', and 'acceptance' on papers and put them on the ground.
4. Add 2–3 empty papers for new voices that may arise.
5. Let every person from the group look at the words ('differences', 'conflicts', etc.) and choose the position s/he wants to occupy, following their intuition.
6. Allow them to speak the voices of this worldly system and watch without interruption.
7. Let them move between positions freely, to represent them and speak their voices.
8. If any voice is compelled to reply to the other, allow him/her to do so freely, without judgments.
9. Observe your inner talk while the process is going. If you feel a new role/emotion/value is needed occupy one of the empty papers, say so.
10. Ask the members to move from wherever they are and occupy the seven continents.
11. Ask every voice representing each continent about their needs to get closer to "Love and peace".
12. Write on a board all those needs, suggestions, solutions…etc.
13. Start writing the needs of continents in a bigger scale, then move down to societies, then families and individuals. Write all their needs.

14. Ask what can be done and how individuals can contribute. Write it on the board.
15. Map individuals' actions, beliefs, thoughts and behaviours to the world.
16. Repeat this exercise with as many people as you can. Think about actions you will take to contribute to building a happier world, starting with yourself, family, colleagues and friends. And remember that every brick matters.

In order to achieve our mission of living in a happier, more cohesive, loving and peaceful world, every human being must take the responsibility to do whatever they can to cultivate inner tranquillity, infusing peace in the emotional field of their relationships with others and everything around. We need to improve our tolerance to experience the new and accept tough emotions that hit us when we experience new things, like thoughts, beliefs and external circumstances. We need to learn the information that comes with them and follow the learning with congruent actions.

The world is programmed to work through emergency rooms. When there is a problem, they give it a quick fix. Not many people pay attention to prevention strategies. And when they do, they limit them to particular areas of life or follow unsustainable ones. This only agitates the system with more anger and suppressed emotions. We need to heal wounds before they get deeper and the emotional voice gets louder.

Practices to save the world are mostly working on separate pieces of the system, each one alone, without paying attention to the complexity of its interconnection as we jump from one level to the other. Each level affects the whole system even if it is considered minor. We need to follow a collective approach that starts with individuals and ends with the whole world.

It is important to follow a wiser approach that respects human minds and intuition instead of suppressing their voices or manipulating them. We need to give them room for expression and listen deeply to the information these voices bring, to benefit individuals and the whole system. We can allow individuals who come up with the problem to suggest solutions. They are the ones who are most experienced in it.

Understand that when different systems come into contact, they may choose to start a war against each other, out of intolerance of differences and the desire for conformity. This is a lose-lose situation. Or they may choose to empathize and accept each other, enabling them to work out a win-win situation.

When we love everything in our lives, we get love multiplied. Finding something to appreciate about even those things that bother us in life (e.g., a friend, job, home, spouse, sibling....) and thinking about it during the day directs our minds to focus on what we love and magnifies it. We start linking this person/thing/situation with loving feelings, and we choose loving actions towards them. Things start shifting in the physical realm. That will help in saving our world from hatred and wars, and our societies from addiction, crime, violence, suicide, and torn families. By healing it with loving peace and peaceful love.

The Loyal Student
and Her Legacy

"A teacher introduces us to a new vision of life,
to make us as sharp as a knife.
Someone who gives us a new sight, to make us reach
the greatest height, to give us the greatest flight."

— MRIDULIKA GANGULY

*I*n this story you'll be introduced to the most loyal student to a wonderous teacher my eyes have ever seen. Her strong belief in what she learned made her study the patterns of her teacher diligently. She has insisted on making her name last after her and passing her knowledge to the world, with humility, kindness, compassion, and tremendous love. This lady is called Sharon Loeschen. She is the CEO and founder of the Virginia Satir Global Network. I am honoured to be one of this institute's continuous students.

When I interviewed Sharon, I remember telling her "I feel humbled talking to you. I consider you something so big, and someone out of reach", and she replied with tremendous kindness and emphasis "No, I am just a human like you, I have two legs and two hands, just like you". It blew my mind! I wondered; how much better would our world be if more people operated with such a modest attitude from their high positions?

Sharon was studying psychology in a graduate program called "Conjoint Family Therapy", which gave her the privilege to work with families and help them overcome their hurdles. Many years later, she saw an advertisement by Virginia Satir about a four-day workshop, in which she introduced the model of working with people on the spot, rather than teaching theoretical concepts only.

Such teaching was not very common in the 1960s. It was intriguing to Sharon. She decided to attend the workshop. She wanted to learn all the things in her profession as a social worker that she believed were truly needed but not being taught at schools. That four-day workshop was one of the most powerful experiences in Sharon's life. She got to watch Virginia working with families, and saw transformations happening before her eyes.

Sharon was fascinated by Virginia's ability to be fully and lovingly focused on the other person. Her presence was amazing! It was like there was no one else in the world. She would completely be with the person she was working with, in all her senses and all her being. Sharon believes that Virginia looked at people in awe, without judgment, just love and acceptance. She understood that everybody can have some unappealing aspects, yet she believed there was a pure spirit inside them. Her job was to come from her pure spirit, to connect with theirs while working with them.

The effect of such experience was so profound on Sharon, to the point that she took the recordings of the workshop sessions and listened to them over and over. In 1986 she read that Virginia was going to demonstrate working with couples at the University of California in Los Angeles, so she attended.

Her fondness for what Virginia was offering to the world increased day after day. During that event, Virginia announced that the most important thing anybody in the helping field can do to be more effective is to work on themselves. Following that announcement, she offered a month-long intensive training in the Rocky Mountains in Colorado, which she called "training communities". Sharon attended those communities for two summers.

Those summer training communities gathered 90 people from around the world, including counsellors, therapists, psychiatrists, social workers, homemakers, musicians, ...etc. That was the essence of it; anybody who wanted to increase their emotional health and grow was welcome. Every morning Virginia would teach them by lecturing the concepts first and then demonstrating how to apply them.

In the afternoon, she would split the attendees into groups of 30 with three trainers, to practise the growth exercises. In the evening, they would be divided into triads, to look at themselves and start processing. This inner work was so intense, sometimes even difficult, causing some people to feel exhausted. It was the first time Sharon experienced such a thing, as Virginia had invented the whole process.

One time, Virginia wanted to teach the attendees how our natural wholeness can get blocked. She asked for a volunteer and Sharon stepped forward. Virginia asked the group "How many holes do you think Sharon has in her body?". People started counting: eyes are two holes, the nose is one hole, and so forth. Then Virginia said, "Just for fun today, try to figure out how many holes you have in your body". Then she continued, "Do you know that there are about 30,000 holes in your skin? The sensing skin. When Sharon came to the world as a baby, all those holes were opened, and they are holy". In her opinion, humans have many holes, in the form of openings, and they are at the same time holy, meaning sacred.

Then she continued, "But life happens, and people start picking up messages or rules from their family and society, which (metaphorically speaking) plugs these holes". Like, for example, it is not okay to talk about what you see and hear in the family. It is not okay to feel, so stop crying! There is nothing to cry about, if you keep crying you know what will happen… but how can people stop crying when they feel upset and their hearts hurt?! Other rules might be that women are not allowed to get angry, that men are not supposed to feel afraid or sad. What this will do is cause people to shut off, because they don't have full use of themselves. They are not seeing, not expressing and not feeling.

To regain their sense of self-worth and wholeness, they need to become aware of those messages. They need to know about the rules they have unconsciously absorbed and been living with, but that are not serving them anymore. What Virginia did was help people to forget those rules and release them to the past. She helped them to have full freedom to see and express themselves, feel whatever they want to feel, and take risks on their own behalf. That is the powerful tool of the five freedoms, to teach people to regain the emotional freedom with which they were born.

Virginia travelled all over the world to teach those freedoms and show their effect on human inner transformation towards their truth, as spirits free from constraints. When those five freedoms are applied, they change the world around us. This was one of the wired moments for Sharon, yet it was an interesting learning that opened her awareness about the type of rules she experienced in her own family. It emphasized her belief that she was standing in front of an unusual human being, one for whom she held tremendous respect.

After attending those summer communities, Sharon got the right formally to teach Virginia's work. Three months later, Virginia died, and Sharon was invited to her ceremony. She decided to write about Virginia's process, to pass it to the following generations of therapists and people in the helping field. After Virginia passed away, people were no longer inspired to spend money and make other kinds of sacrifices to attend those summer training communities in the mountains. They were not willing to do it for someone who was not Virginia Satir.

And so, Sharon took the lead to teach Virginia's knowledge in Virginia's way. She kept reading, studying, and applying Virginia's work, relentlessly. She spent thousands of hours looking at her work and came up with what she calls "The roadmap of Virginia's process for change in families". This became the basis and focus of her life's work ever since.

Sharon was only a student to Virginia, one who knew her from a distance. She was not her friend, but she watched Virginia's work so attentively and that meant a lot to her. Virginia's work was so different from the kind of remote clinical work, that Sharon had with her professors before. It was different because Virginia was there connecting with the person with all her senses. That is what inspired Sharon to continue the legacy of Virginia, to pass and teach her work to others.

Sharon is very happy to see how many people around the globe have embraced the concepts of our great role model and mother of practical family therapy. Professionals are even offering their services to non-profit organizations, to teach people how to work on emotional problems using Virginia's tools in ways consistent with their religion. It makes her feel that this material is non-volatile. It will last for generations to come, which was her dream when she first founded the "Virginia Satir Global Network".

Many people can't afford therapy or are unwilling to visit a therapist, yet they will consult a coach to get an education about emotions. Coaching and being coached has been a popular trend for some time; it is a way to keep Virginia's knowledge alive in people's minds and hearts. Because she is simply teaching people to return to their humanity! I salute Virginia, and Sharon for keeping Virginia's legacy alive in us, the legacy of love and peace, leading us to endless happiness.

Sharon L. the loyal student & teacher

My hope for the world is to see a collective desire for change and to see heroes everywhere, advocates for kindness, love, and acceptance. Rather than confining the ripple of love, we will help it to grow. And now, as we reach the end of the story of building a happier world with love, what is the very first loving action you will take as an individual, as part of a couple, a family and a society to make this mission complete? I trust your wise heart and leave the choice of the best action to you.

Conclusion

This book has been about developing peace from the inside, by cultivating love to all parts of our personality. That includes the parts we dislike as much as those we like. These might be physical, intellectual or emotional parts. By now you are equipped with the tools necessary to show love to these parts and can thus make choices to develop the inner tranquillity that allows you to take new actions, to bring you more happiness.

After cultivating self-love and reclaiming your lost passions or developing new ones, you are ready to bond with another person with love, to build a happy healthy family. In this bond you will be a loving parent, raising loving human beings who will become loving children, friends, siblings, colleagues, and neighbours living in a society where they give and receive love freely.

I have seen common patterns in my coaching practice. All are rooted in one way or another to a deficiency in love. Whatever the situation, the antidote has always been the same. We have had to go to that little child to help him/her feel more safe and secure, to know that all is okay and will be okay. We taught that little child to develop more compassion towards the self, events, and other people in his/her life. This compassion takes the form of more love leading to more peace. When this happens, the actions to solve the symptoms come so easily and fluently.

From my many practical coaching sessions – when I was privileged to see amazing souls – I can say with full confidence that whenever there is more love, there will always be more peace. Together we can help build a much happier world, starting with the self. You may think this is a big challenge, wondering if it will work, but I can tell you with unshakable trust that yes, it does work. Once we comprehend this love and give and receive more of it in all aspects of our lives, we reap the fruit of tremendous peace and untraded happiness.

Remember always, that accepting diversity starts at home, when couples accept their diverse worlds and parents tolerate their kids' difference. This can only happen when we accept all our parts as important contributors to our lives. Self-worth results from treating people with love; it is the core of life, and every human being has the right to feel it. Ignoring it is the same as saying "You don't have the right to live or exist on earth". This activates fear, which when suppressed becomes magnified and pushes people to act mindlessly. We need to give it much more attention than it currently receives and treat it with tremendous respect.

In order to start a happy and healthy relationship, you must become a ready soul first, by healing your old wounds and creating a happy life as an individual. Only then you can bridge with love to another ready soul to create a happy family. We live in a blinded, traumatized world. A lot of hidden emotional and physical hurt is practised under beautified words like 'professionalism', 'official', 'formal', etc. People have forgotten that a major aspect of humankind creation is our emotions – and that unforeseen wounds are created when these emotions are treated as something unpleasant or undesired.

All human beings have five birthright freedoms to exercise. The freedom to see and hear what is going on instead of what should be, was or will be; the freedom to feel all kinds of emotions; the freedom to express their thoughts and emotions; the freedom to ask for what they want instead of always waiting for permission; and the freedom to take risks on their own behalf. When these freedoms are exercised equally, with the right support system, wisdom and tolerance, a lot of worldly suffering will disappear.

People are hurting each other out of fear. That fear results from a lack of self-worth, from feeling threatened at their core; it pushes them to take actions that go against human nature. Yet they deny this truth, because doing so protects their self-worth from being affected again; it keeps feelings of guilt or regret from coming to the surface.

By reading this book, pondering and reflecting, and doing all exercises several times, you are undertaking a rebirth process. This rebirth is necessary to rescue the new generation, even before they are born, from living blindly in collective worldly trauma.

If you are hesitating to invest your time and money in this method, let me ask you: "Which is more important? Money or protecting yourself, your family, your friends and your children from facing violence? Which will consume more time? Preventing wars in your inner and outer world, due to love deficiency, or dealing with consequences after they happen?". The choice is yours, and I trust your decision.

Make sure to book your complimentary coaching session with me, to help you get the most out of this book and the things that came up for you while reading it. I am passionate about developing a happier and more peaceful world, and I love working with individuals who wish to join me on this journey.

References

Hill, N. (2007). *Think and grow rich*. E-book, www.think-and-grow-rich-eBook.com

McGraw, P. (2001). *Self-Matters*. New York, Simon & Schuster.

Loeschen, S. (2005). *Enriching your relationship with self and others*. Burien, Washington, AVANTA The Virginia Satir Network.

Satir, V. (2011). *Making Contact*. Madison, Wisconsin, Halcyon Publishing Design.

Chapman, G. (2011). *The 5 love languages*. IL, Chicago, Northfield Publishing.

The John Gottman Institute, https://www.gottman.com

Norwood, R. (2008). *Women who love too much*. New York, Simon & Schuster.

Hendricks, G. & Hendricks, K. (2015). *Conscious loving ever after*. London, UK, Hay House.

Levine, P. (1997). *Waking the tiger: Healing trauma*. Berkeley, California, North Atlantic Books.

Mindell, A. (2014). *Sitting in the Fire*. Deep Democracy Exchange.

Archuleta, K. & Lutter, S. (2020). Utilizing family systems theory in financial therapy. Wiley Online Library.

Author Biography

I work closely with clients who:

- Feel rejected and confused
- Are engaged and feeling hesitant about this major change in their lives
- Are newly married (up to three years) and finding it difficult to sustain the same level of happiness and joy in the relationship that once existed
- Feel stressed and confused while dealing with their teenage son/daughter.

I help my clients to:

- Release their emotional burdens from toxic relationships and an unhappy history
- Regain their self-love and peace
- Let go of frustration
- Define how they want their relationships to look and feel
- Write a new loving story
- Set up healthier boundaries, and
- Have the happy relationship they want.

My coaching helps clients reduce frustration in their relationships. They start feeling more hopeful, calmer and happier. It helps them eliminate negativity and start becoming more proactive, rather than being reactive and complaining. They become more focused and positive with regard to their relationships and start making better choices.

I am an accredited and certified relationship coach. I have coached 140+ hours with 50+ clients. I have long working experience in different fields, and 200+ official training hours in NLP, hypnosis and Relationships Coaching.

My rich and diverse background helps me connect with and understand my clients on a uniquely deep and empathetic level. I appreciate the uniqueness of every person and their life journey as they work to create meaningful change. I work with my clients as a partner and help them find relief, acceptance and self-awareness while working towards building happier, healthier and loving relationships.